By: Reverend Doctor Antwon C. Lewis, Ph.D.

"Ministerial Ethics:

It's Purpose and Importance in 21st Century Ministry"

Acknowledgements

Giving all honor to God, the most high and the Creator of all mankind, I am most grateful and humbled for this opportunity to write *"as I pursue greater in my life."* I am eternally grateful to God for the gifts and the abilities He has placed within me. While a completed dissertation bears the single name of the student, the process which led to its completion is always accomplished with the dedicated contributions and work of other people. I wish to acknowledge and show appreciation to those individuals who have supported me in this endeavor.

To my children: *Hezekiah, Josiah and Maleigha,* thank you for bringing a young-old man joy in the midst of trials.

To *my Mother*, *my Champion* and *Mentor*, *Eatherene B. Lewis*, I love you so much for you have been with me through the ups and downs of life; thank you for never giving up on me. Thanks Dad for just being you. To my brothers and sisters: *Thomas, Tracy, Meoisha, Jessica* and *Monte'*, thanks to you guys and girls for being who you are to me.

To my *Aunts* and *God Aunts* especially Lelia B. Jackson and Ella Mae Brown you all are the world's greatest aunts. To my cousins, you guys and girls are too many to name, but know that I love each of you. You Rock!

To my friend(s): Erica D. Sutton-Dowling, Dr. James N. Davis, III, Sister Angill Warren, Sister Georgell R. Pierson, Missionary Michelle Searcy, Sister Louise Willis, Deacon Mario Wilkerson, Dr. Erta C. Livingston Jr., William Matthew Griggs, Brother Minister Michael Blanton, Spencer Whitaker, thanks for knowing that I would pursue and press forward. Lastly, but not least to my close and dear friend James W. Holcomb III, my appreciation and thanks to you run deep – for you stuck with me and advised the whole way through.

Biography

Dr. Antwon C. Lewis is a man of diligence and excellence, constantly embracing opportunities to be a blessing to others. As a child, growing up in Holy Rock Reformed Episcopal Church, Willington, South Carolina, Dr. Lewis received the Holy Ghost at the very tender age of 13. Immediately following this experience, his Christian foundation of prayer, faith, and service with a glad heart grew. Upon harkening to the voice of God, he begin to work diligently and serve faithfully at Holy Rock Reformed Episcopal Church under the leadership of the Right Reverend Eugene Sims until departure into the military. Under his leadership, Dr. Lewis served in the following capacities: Sunday school teacher, youth rap session secretary, youth choir president, church musician and toured Germany at age of 16 as a missionary/ representative for the Diocese of the Southeast of the Reformed Episcopal Church.

After graduating from Calhoun Falls High School in 1998, Dr. Lewis went on to attend Piedmont Technical College and Lander University, all while working full time at the old Milliken Plant and serving in the church. In 2001, Dr. Lewis went on establish career of military service in the United State Army.

A strong advocate for education and personal progress, Dr. Lewis has earned a Bachelor's of Science in Applied Management from Grand Canyon University, and both a Masters of Arts in Christian Counseling and a Doctor of Philosophy in Pastoral Ministry from Atlantic Coast Theological Seminary. Dr. Lewis is also a certified member of the American Association of Christian Counselors.

Dr. Lewis resides in New Brockton, Alabama and is the devoted father of his "two little men," Master Hezekiah C. Lewis and Master Josiah C. Lewis and his daughter, Maleigha Lewis - who bring him much joy and are the sole motivation behind his achievements and success. Dr. Lewis is an ordained Elder in the Church of God in Christ, Inc., and serves on the ministerial staff of New Jerusalem COGIC in Enterprise, Alabama under the tutelage and leadership of Superintendent William K. Ellison.

Thesis Topic:
Understanding the importance and purpose of ethics in ministry as
it pertains to minister, pastors, and all Christian leaders. What is ethics?
"Christian ethics is the study of good and evil, right and wrong. What
constitutes good, virtuous, healthy character? How does one discern and
do the right thing in various ethical dilemmas?"

Research Title:
The origin of Christian ethics is Christianity. Ethical practices for
Christians are founded on solid theology-the sovereignty of God, the
lordship of Christ, and the new righteousness possible in the new
kingdom. Unlike philosophic ethics, Christian character can never be
separated from its religious nature. It is connected it with God, being
interpersonal, future-oriented, and universally applicable.

Reasons for the Study:

The determining factor of what is right and wrong leads to in-depth for study of ethics. The moral principles of those in ministry must be influenced by scriptural standards. Many Christians and ministers alike often determine right and wrong by their own value system. Those in

ordained ministry must align themselves with scriptural standards in order effectively to work for God.

Relevance of Study:

Living in a day and age, where ethical behavior is not always valued there is a growing need for ministerial ethics. Even in the corporate sector many executives in today's society value the bottom line over ethics. There is one profession, though, where unethical behavior should never appear-in ministry. Those who have been called to preach the gospel should exhibit a lifestyle of godliness and integrity.

ABSTRACT

Studying the differentiations among various ministerial ethics and the necessity of understanding and developing ethical practices in ministry as pertains to the 21st century ministry. There is a nature of the crisis in ministerial ethics today. It can be seen in the following areas: false sense of spirituality, a false sense of evaluation of ministry, and a false sense of expectations in post modernism of today's ministry. Many times spiritual ministry is easy to counterfeit. Oftentimes, clergy makes the mistakes preaching and teaching with little or no study. Therefore the demands and pressures of life and time constraints leads many to plagiarized sermons, lessons and objectives. Theological articles are copied without credit, or even worse, proclaimed as one's own effort. Ministers, who speak for God, devote little time to prayer and meditation, in speaking to God. One is lead to believe that there are unethical and immoral pursues to ministry.

Therefore, the need to research and offer ways in compounding the crises within the contemporary society. This does not devalue genuine ministry, although outward appearances and external appearances can offer circumstances. The rapid transitions of contemporary society have blurred definitions of ministry. In fact, today's world often measures ministry by worldly standards. This encourages hypocrisy and the lack of ministerial integrity. Ministry is in ethical crisis. Heightening dilemmas is the fact the crisis is generally unseen, even by many church leaders and ministers.

TABLE OF CONTENTS

Introduction .... page xii

Chapter One: Defining of Ethics

Statement of the Problem... page 1
Importance of the Study... page 2
Determining what is Right and Wrong .... page 4
Definition of Four Areas of Ethics.................................... page 7
Simple Review of Four Areas of Ethics .... page 8
Chapter Two: Why Ministry Ethics
History of the Study/ Nature of Crisis .... page 16
What is at Stake for the Church & World........................... page 17
Deeper Look at What Ministry Ethics Entails .... page 18
Ministry Decorum & Etiquette .... page 18
Differentiation of Manners .... page 21
Spiritual Disciplines... page 25
Chapter Three: The Process of Teaching and Learning
What is Theology .... page 28
The Importance of the Theory of Free Will....................... page 38
The Importance of the Theory of Consciousness and
     Unconsciousness... page 44
Suggestions for Recovering Ethical Ministry .... page 53
Recovering the Minister... page 54
Recovering the Church .... page 55
Strategic Systems of Recovery .... page 58
Chapter Four: Commissioned with Resources from Christ
Gentile Conversion .... page 81
Important Issues in the Non-Pauline Churches.................. page 86
Commissioned with Resources from Christ & the Call of the
     Ministry.. page 91
Your Daily Walk as a Minister .... page 94
Identity of Chris .... page 96
A Will within a Will .... page 98
Servant Leadership.. page 104
The Minister's Alliance to the Ministry............................. page 109

Chapter Five: Summary and Conclusions

Mentoring Program for Ministry & Ministerial Ethics...................page 123
Leadership Development ....page 123
Spiritual Formation ....page 133
Summary & Conclusion..page 161
Questionnaire ....page 182
Bibliography ....page 185

INTRODUCTION

Ethical behavior is decreasingly valued we all must employ guidelines and principles. Although, newspaper headlines and the evening news reveal the scandals brought about by their unethical behaviors; ministers and Christian leaders must have integrity. Ministers and Christian leaders learn more about the character and ways of God, while constantly seeking opportunities to embracing the life changing principles.

In the process of interaction with the world, the opportunity to receive diverse information from the environment permits to pursuit this research of studies. Yet faced with many obstacles and trials, to embrace greater from within and preserve is imperative. It is understood that a man does not create his ideas, but ideas create the man. Therefore, the determining factor of what is right and wrong leads to reasons for study. Christian leaders, right and wrong must be influenced by scriptural standards. Many Christians and ministers alike often determine right and wrong by their own value system. To simply study God is in and of itself unfruitful and rudimentary without application to the daily life of the believer.

Chapter One Defining Ethics

Statement of Problem

We must recognize the biblical foundations of Christian ethics. Some wonder whether an ethical lifestyle is still possible in a postmodern world that questions the validity of the moral and spiritual foundation of postmodern. "Hauerwas observes that Christian ethics is being called to exist in a fragmented and violent world. Absolutes are still needed in a world that has largely discarded them."[1]

The privatization of religion has made ethical behavior fragile. There is a need for renewed truth in Christian conviction. It is impossible to function with abstract sense of ethics. A familiar behavioral model says behaviors are based on values, and which in return are based on the principles or beliefs comprise one's worldview. The theological base of Christian behavior is comprised by the current ethical crisis.

"Some maintain that our world needs to redefine ethics lest morality and virtue disappear from society completely."[2] No doubt we

---

[1] Moore, G.E. Principia Ethica (1903) Cambridge University Press revised edition ISBN 052144848)
[2] Ibid

exist in a world where postmodernism has shaken loose much that was formerly nailed down. We must identify a normative ethic of doing and being in which questions about the biblical foundation of our behaviors we can establish or reestablish moral norms, obligations and values.

Ideas of how Christianity can address the worldview it is the desire of clergymen, Christian Apologists and Christians to help the community while influencing society. The Church universal does not rise above its moral standards. The church must reclaim her authority in teaching continuing to provide the necessary spiritual nourishment. The present-day church of modern influencing has succumbed to bottleneck spirituality. Also, the church prohibits her from pouring itself out into the lives of a needy world; the bottleneck is at the top. Spiritual leadership must be prevalent and in affect. It is understood that virtue influences choices, goals, roles and behavior.

Importance of Study

The significance of the crisis may be identified by asking, "What is at stake for the minister, the church, and the world?" Much is a stake for those who preach and minister. Understanding how and why minister's act certain ways is not easy because humans are prone to rationalization often leading to personalities and power struggles. Honest self-evaluation becomes increasingly difficult. We must admit that hard questions exist, identify them, and encourage personal reflection.

Ministry is not limited to full-time ministers or church workers. Interest in ministerial ethics expands too many professionals and volunteers who serve the church in a ministerial capacity: elders, deacons, pastors, pastoral administrators, pastoral care ministers, spiritual directors, youth ministers, campus ministers, directors of religious education, and teachers. As the secular world gives increased attention to professional ethics, those in ministry must not lag behind.

While ethics and etiquette are connected, ethics in ministry is ultimately about integrity. Integrity is performing at your best at all times, whether someone is around or not. What is at stake is the integrity of ministry. How can those who are not whole help others toward wholeness? Effective ministry does not demand perfection; it demands integrity.

No subject is more relevant for ministry than exploring how truth, beliefs and values integrate in Christian living. No ministry can be faithful if it does not help people toward righteous living through the ethical challenges of our time. Minister must do more that guide others toward ethical behaviors; they must be examples. Ethical standards apply to all Christians, but spiritual leaders have a higher degree of ethical accountability.

Ministerial ethics is a religious code of behavior that is grounded in biblical truth. The ethical codes for the Assemblies of God, the Church of the Nazarene, or the Baptist church might be different for each denomination. Usually ethical religious codes define a particular group, profession, or an individual. If a person does not have a code of ethics, he presumes to have a license to behave in any manner he chooses.

Determining what is Right and Wrong

People determine what is right and wrong by their own personal value system. The Christian values system is influenced by scriptural standards, and how we apply scriptural truth to our lives. Reflecting on this thought, it may be concluded that personal understanding is not new and unique, but they are simply a collection of what is read, hear, experienced, felt and dreamt of. So, in the process of interaction with the world, we receive diverse information from the environment, resulting in accepting or rejecting these ideas. Some of the thoughts recess in our mind and combine with other concepts that represent a part of us. Thus, we develop new ideas that give us a different way to perceive reality. However, we sometimes ask ourselves; do I really need an explanation for every event, experience, and feeling? Do not I devaluate the world by trying to find words that can explain its meaning finally, is our dictionary rich enough to describe the essence of nature of our being? Moreover, why do not we just feel experience, and interact with the environment than think of, explain, and analyze our lives.

As children, we have been reared to not just live, but to live everyday with of meaning and significance. Each day one lives he or she must learn something from that day to carry to the next day. If we live and never learn then our living is in vain. Life itself is a gift and it should be nurtured. Anything worth having is worth working for. We are often plagued with the idea of who we are and what is our purpose. Our purpose can be found in our experiences as well as our past failures and accomplishments. Situations does not define us, they only enable us to achieve more. Without the proper situation refinement cannot be easily pursued.

Only when one releases his or her self to God can purpose be found. Rejection seems to be a moment of despair to many of us. Once we feel rejected then we are able to soul search within. We then begin to question the rejections; the source of rejection comes from pain. When one is rejected he or she automatically feels alienated. Alienation as we know it is a separation from an individual and or a group of people. Though pain is felt through the separation we must remember that Jesus is right there by our side. It is only by the heavenly Father's permission that these experiences occur, to focus on Him in order to discover our purpose. We cannot become over consumed with ideas and carnal ideologies and be driven away from the scripture and its effectiveness. God is our strength as long as we look for Him; He will always be there.

Situational ethics offers the logical as long it does not hurt anyone it is OK. This teaching is doing great damage to the church. In some instances, the majority of laity or laymen believe in situational ethic rather than moral ethics. If pastors and leaders do not address this ethical dilemma, as well as, live by obvious moral ethics, they contribute to the dilemma themselves.

Ethical Areas

Ethics reflect who a person-his conduct, his innermost thoughts, his speaking, teaching and lifestyle. Ethics for Christianity differ from secular ethics because Christianity is linked to the Bible and determined by the unchanging truth of Holy Scripture. "Ethics, also known as moral philosophy, is a branch philosophy that involves systematizing, defending and recommending concepts of right and wrong conduct. The term comes from the Greek word ethos, which means "character". Ethics is a complement to Aesthetics in the philosophy field of Axiology. In philosophy, ethics studies the moral behavior in humans and how one should act. Ethics may be divided into four major areas study:"

Meta-ethics[3], about the theoretical meaning and reference of moral propositions and how their truth values (if any) may be determined;

---

[3] Moore, G.E. Principia Ethica (1903) Cambridge University Press revised edition ISBN 052144848)

Normative ethics[4], about the practical means of determining a moral course of action; (discipline)

Applied ethics[5]; about how moral outcomes can be achieved in specific situations;

Descriptive ethics[6], also known as comparative ethic, is the study of people's about morality;

Ethics seek to resolve questions dealing with human morality concepts such as good and evil, right and wrong, virtue and vice justice, as well as crime.

Ethical Areas of Ethics

Meta-Ethics[7]

"Meta-ethics is afield within philosophy that seeks to understand the nature normative ethics. The focus of meta-ethics is on how we

---

[4] Ibid
[5] Ibid
[6] Ibid
[7] Moore, G.E. Principia Ethica (1903) Cambridge University Press revised edition ISBN 052144848)

understand, know about, and what we mean when we talk about what is right and what is wrong."

Meta-ethics has always accompanied philosophical ethics, but in this explicit sense it came to the fore with *G. E. Moore's Principia Ethica* from 1903. In it he first wrote about what he called the "naturalistic fallacy". Moore was seen to reject naturalism in ethics, in his "Open Question Argument. This made thinkers look again at second order questions about ethics. Earlier, the Scottish philosopher David Hume had put forward a similar view on the difference between facts and values."

Studies of how we know in ethics divided into cognitivism and non-cognitivism; this is similar to the contrast between descriptivist and no descriptivist's. Non-cognitivism is the claim that when we judge something as right and wrong, this is neither true nor false. We may for example be only expressing our emotional feelings about these things. Cognitvism can then be seen as the claim that when we talk about right and wrong, we are talking about matters of fact.

The ontology of ethics is about value-bearing things or properties, i.e. the kind of things or stuff referred to by ethical propositions. Nondescriptivist's and non-cognitivists believe that ethics does not need a specific ontology, since ethical propositions do not refer. This is known as an anti-realist position. Realists on the other hand must explain what kind of entities, properties or states are relevant for ethics, how they have value, and why they guide and motivate our actions.

Normative Ethics[8]

Normative ethics is the study of ethical action. It is the branch of philosophical ethics that investigates the set of questions that arise when considering how one ought to act, morally speaking. Normative ethics is distinct from meta-ethics because it examines standards for the rightness and wrongness of actions, while meta-ethics studies the meaning of moral language and the metaphysics of moral facts.

Normative ethics is also distinct from descriptive ethics, as the latter is an empirical investigation of people's moral beliefs. To put it another way, descriptive ethics would be concerned with determining what proportion of people believe that killing is always wrong, while normative

---

[8] Moore, G.E. Principia Ethica (1903) Cambridge University Press revised edition ISBN 052144848)

ethics is concerned with whether it is correct to hold such a belief. Hence, normative ethics is sometimes called prescriptive, rather that descriptive. However, on certain versions of the meta-ethical view called moral realism, moral facts are both descriptive and prescriptive at the same time.

Broadly speaking, normative ethics can be divided into the sub disciplines of moral theory and applied ethics. In recent years, the boundaries between these sub-disciplines have increasingly been dissolving as moral theorists become more interested in applied problems and applied ethics is becoming more profoundly philosophically informed. Traditional moral theories rest on principles that determine whether an action is right or wrong. Classical theories in this vein included utilitarianism, Kantianism, and some forms of contractarianism. These theories offered overarching moral principles to use to resolve difficult moral decisions.

Applied Ethics[9]

Applied ethics is the philosophical examination, from a moral standpoint, of particular issues in private and public life that are matters of moral judgment. It is thus to use philosophical methods to identify the morally correct course of action in various fields of human life. Bioethics, for an example, is concerned with identifying the correct approach to matters such as euthanasia, or the allocation of scare health resources, or the use of human embryos in research.. Environmental ethics is concerned with questions such as the duties of duty of whistleblowers to the general public as opposed to their loyalty to their employers. As such, it is an area of professional philosophy that is well paid and highly valued both within and outside of academia.

Applied ethics distinguished from normative ethics, which concerns what people should believe to be right and wrong, and from meta-ethics, which concerns the nature of moral statements. An emerging

---

[9] Moore, G.E. Principia Ethica (1903) Cambridge University Press revised edition ISBN 052144848)

typology for applied ethics uses seven domains to help improve organizations and social issues at the nation and global level:

Decision ethics, or ethical theories and ethical decision processes

Profession ethics or ethics to improve professionalism

Clinical ethics or ethics to improve our basic health needs'

    i.   Business ethics, Or individual based morals to improve ethics in an organization

   ii.   Organizational ethics, or ethics among organizations

  iii.   Social ethics or ethics among nation and as one global unit

  iv.   Sexual ethics, or ethics based around sexual acts

Descriptive Ethics[10]

Descriptive ethics, also known as comparative ethics, is study of people's beliefs about morality. It contrast with prescriptive or normative ethics, which is the study of ethical theories that prescribe how people

---

[10] Moore, G.E. Principia Ethica (1903) Cambridge University Press revised edition ISBN 052144848)

ought to act, and with metha-ethics, which is the study of what ethical terms and theories actually refer to.

Descriptive ethics is a form of empirical research into the attitudes of individuals or groups of people. Those working on descriptive ethics aim to uncover people's beliefs about such things as values, which actions are right and wrong, and which characteristics of moral agents are virtuous. Research into descriptive ethics may also investigate people ethical ideals or what actions societies condemn or punish in law. What ought to be noted is that culture is generational and static. Therefore a new generation will come with its own set of morals and that qualifies to be their ethics. Descriptive ethics will hence try to oversee whether ethics still holds its place in a new generation. Because descriptive ethics involves empirical investigation, it is a field that is usually investigated by those working in the field of evolutionary biology, psychology, sociology or anthropology. Information that comes from descriptive ethics is, however, also used an in philosophical arguments.

Chapter Two: Why Ministry Ethics?

An ethical crisis exists in ministry. Some days it seems as if religious people are not all that religious. With sexual scandals and abuses, homosexuality, and financial irregularities frequently in the news, the world sees a growing ethical problem. Of greater concerns are the less visible ethical issues that tempt ministers daily in their choices, goals, and obligations.

The growing ethical crisis in ministry is seen in the increasing number of resources. Twenty years ago ministerial ethics was seldom discussed. Today, a quick survey of the Web reveals hundreds of sites with policy statements, disclaimers, and the resources for ministerial ethics. When ethics is defined and it theological foundations are reviewed; we can formulate reasons why the crisis is important. The nature of the crisis –its internal and external contributing factors-and informed suggestions for recovering ethical ministry based on biblical foundation also need the ministers' consideration.

The ethical crisis is not limited to ministry. Our nation is in a moral crisis. The crisis in ministerial ethic is part of a larger moral crisis in nation. The crisis in ministry is evident in three main areas-false spirituality, false evaluation of ministry, false expectations on the part of the ministers; churches; and the world. Spiritual ministry is easy to counterfeit. Preachers preach and teach with little or no study. Time pressure encourages plagiarized sermons and classes. Bulletin articles are copied without credit, or worse, set forth as one's own effort. Ministers' speed too little time in prayer, in speaking to God; in listening to God, all in the name of speaking for God. Some involved in ministry covertly pursue unethical, immoral lifestyles.

Compounding the crisis, our contemporary society does not appreciate that genuine ministry is not dependent on outward appearances nor external circumstances. The rapid transitions of contemporary society have blurred definitions of ministry. In fact, todays' world often measures ministry by worldly standards. This encourages hypocrisy and the lack of ministerial integrity. Ministry is in ethical crisis. Heightening the dilemma is the fact that crisis is generally unseen, by many church leaders and ministers.

What is at stake for the church?

Churches seldom rise above the moral standards and teaching of the person who regularly provides spiritual nourishment. If the modern church faces a spiritual bottleneck that prohibits the church from pouring itself out into the lives of a needy world, the bottleneck is at the top. The church needs spiritual leadership that incarnated the life of Jesus before it can understand the challenge of living out the life of Jesus in our world. Virtue influences our choices, goals, roles, and behaviors. Genuine virtue connects faith and behavior. Virtue is a lifetime endeavor. Christian morality is not built solely on keeping rules. Christians shaped by the church community should have a moral shape.

What is at stake for the church may be summarized in three questions: Will we be spiritual or secular? Will we be God's presence in this world with a clear word from God, or merely another siren song? Well we are light and salt?

One need only observe the catastrophe of ministers gone astray to recognize how closely the world is watching those who claim to follow Jesus, especially those who serve in ministry. For the world, salvation, eternity, the gospel, public morality and ultimately society itself is at stake.

Society functions and is safe because a level of morality prevails. Generally my neighbors do not seek to robe me, kill me or take advantage of me. I am safe in society because a prevailing moral standard. However, increased random violence marks the decay of generally accepted moral standards. Prison populations swell. The dignity of human life is diminished in a variety of ways.

Ministry Decorum/Etiquette

What is Etiquette?

Etiquette is a code of behavior that delineates expectations for social behavior according to contemporary conventional norms within a society, social class or group. The French word etiquette, literally signifying a tag or label, was used in a modern sense in English around 1750. From the

1500s through the early 1900s, children learned etiquette at school. Etiquette has changed and evolved over the years.

Etiquette in terms of Culture

Etiquette is depending on culture; what is excellent etiquette in one society may shock another. Etiquette can vary widely between different cultures and nations. For example, in Hausa culture, eating while standing may be seen as offensively casual and ill-omened behavior, insulting the host's and showing a lack of respect for the scarcity of food-the offense is known as "eating with the devil" or "committing santi." In China, a person who takes the last item o food from a common plate or bowl without first offering it to others at the table may be seen at a glutton who is insulting the host's generosity. Traditionally, if guests do not have leftover food in front of them at the end of a meal, it is to the dishonor of the host. In America a guest is expect to eat all of the food given to them, as a compliment to the quality of the cooking. However, it is still considered polite to offer food from a common plate or bowl to others at the table.

In such rigid hierarchal cultures as Korea and Japan, alcohol helps to break down the strict social barrier between classes. It allows for a hint of informality to creep in. It is traditional for host and guest to take turn filling each other's cups and encouraging each other to gulp it down. For someone who does not consume alcohol (except for religious reasons), it can be difficult escaping the ritual of the social drink. Etiquette is a topic that has occupied writers and thinkers in all sophisticated societies for millennia, beginning with a behavior code by Ptahhotep, a vizier in ancient Egypt's Old Kingdom during the reign of the Fifth Dynasty king Djedkare Isesi (ca. 2414-2375 BC). All known literate civilizations, including ancient Greece and Rome, developed rules for proper social conduct. Confucius included rules for eating and peaking along with his more philosophical sayings.

Early modern conceptions of what behavior identifies a "gentleman" were codified in the century, in a book by Baldassare Castiglione, Il Cortegiano ("The Courtier"); it codification of expectations at the court Urbino remained in force in its essentials until World War I. Louis XIV established an elaborate and rigid court ceremony, but distinguished himself from the by Giovanni della Casa; in fact, in Italian, etiquette is generally called galateo (or ethichetta or proctocollo).

In the American colonies Benjamin Franklin and George Washington wrote codes of conduct for young gentlemen. The immense popularity of advice columns and books by Letitia Baldrige and Miss Manners shows the currency of this topic. Even more recently, the rise of the Internet has necessitated the adaptation of existing rules of conduct to create Netiquette, which governs the drafting of email, rules for participating in an online forum, and so on.

In Germany, many books dealing with etiquette, especially dining, dressing etc., called the Knigge, named after Adolph Freiherr Knigge who wrote the book about manner and also about the social states of its time, but not about etiquette. Etiquette may be wielded as a social weapon. The outward adoption of the superficial mannerisms of an in-group, in the interests of social advancement rather than a concern for others, is considered by many a form snobbery, lacking in virtue.

Differentiation of manner types

Curtis' also specifically outlines three manner categories; hygiene, courtesy and cultural norms, each of which help to account for the multifaceted role manners play in society. These categories are based on the outcome rather than the motivation of manner behavior and individual

manner behaviors may fit in to 2 or more categories.

> **Hygiene Manners**-are any manners which affect disease
  transmission. They are likely to be taught at an early age, primarily
  through parental discipline, positive behavioral enforcement
  around continence with bodily fluids (such as toilet training) and
  the avoidance or removal of items that pose a disease rick for
  children. It is expected that, by adulthood, hygiene manners are so
  entrenched in ones' behavior that they become second nature.
  Violations are likely to elicit disgust responses.

> **Courtesy Manners**-demonstrate one's ability to put the interests
  of others before oneself; to display self-control and good intent for
  the purposes of being trusted in social interactions. Courtesy
  manners help to maximize the benefits of group living by
  regulating social interaction. Disease avoidance behavior can
  sometimes be compromised in the performance of courtesy
  manners. They may be taught in the same way as hygiene manners
  but are likely to also be learned through direct, indirect (i.e.

Observing the interactions of others) or imagined (i.e. through the executive functions of the brain) social interactions. The learning of courtesy manners may take place at an older age than hygiene manners, because individuals must have at least some means of communication and some awareness of self and social positioning. The violation of courtesy manners most commonly results in social disapproval from peers.

➤ **Cultural Norm Manners**-typically demonstrates one's identity within a specific socio-cultural group. Adherence to culture norm manners allows for the demarcation of socio-identities and the creation of boundaries which inform who is to be trusted or who to be deemed as 'other'. Cultural norm manners are learnt through the enculturation and reutilization of 'the familiar' and through exposure to 'otherness' or those who are identified as foreign or different. Transgressions and non-adherence to cultural normal manners commonly result in alienation. Cultural norms, by their very nature, have a high level of between-group variability but are likely to be common to all those who identify with a given group identity.

➢ **Rules of etiquette-** encompass most aspects of social interaction in any society, though the term itself is not commonly used. A rule of etiquette may reflect an underlying ethical code, or it may reflect a person's fashion or status. Rules of etiquette are usually unwritten, but aspects of etiquette have been codified from time to time.

Protocol

There are two meaning of the word protocol. In the legal sense, it is defined as an international agreement that supplements or amends of a treaty. In the diplomatic sense, the term refers to the set of rules, procedures, conventions and ceremonies that relate to relations between states. In general, protocol represents the recognized and generally accepted system of international courtesy.

The term protocol is derived from the Greek word protokollan (first glue). This comes from the act of gluing a sheet of paper to the form of a document to preserve it when it was sealed, which imparted additional authenticity to it. In the beginning, the term protocol related to the various forms of interaction observed in official correspondence between states, which were often elaborate in nature. In course of time, however, it has to cover a much wider range of international relations.

Spiritual Disciplines

We as people of God live a life that God can and will be glorified. God has been known to use ordinary people to do extraordinary things. A spiritual discipline in Christianity is an exercise of events in which an individual practice a closer walk with God. However, the spiritual disciplines can be best seen in those persons who walk as Christ walk. There are many examples throughout the Bible of spiritual disciplines. The man and or woman that seek after the things of God will walk and or practice those things that pertain to God just as Christ did. When one knows his or her historical background of their faith they are ensured for a successful walk within their faith. Adam and Eve are the parents of all mankind. Though they fell from God's grace, God provided a way of escape to them. (Genesis 3:7-8)[11] Through their restored efforts God established the invisible church in which we are part of.

---

[11] King James Version. Holy Bible Grand Rapids: Zondervan 2001

Spiritual disciplines are necessary for ministry in the Body of Christ. We are spiritual beings wrapped in flesh commissioned to perform a work for God. To be successful in the work one must first surrender to the mighty hand of God. Upon surrendering one must willing to adhere to the guiding and the leading of the Holy Spirit. During our tenure here on earth we will be met with all forms of snares and obstacles just as those in the early church experienced. The Apostle Paul was a despiser of the faith but later on converted. After Paul's conversion understand that he too must suffered the things he done unto others. (2 Corinthians 11:21-33)[12] As a spiritual discipline, the Apostle Paul was placed in the Roman jail for trying to fulfill his earthly mission. While in jail Paul prayed and Silas song praises to God. This represents one denial of self for the greater good of the call. In order to be successful spiritual discipline spiritual habits must practice daily and implemented in one's life.

Spiritual disciplines and spiritual formation must work together. They are in relationship to one another. Spiritual disciplines can exist in one's life but spiritual formation does not necessary be in one's life.

---

[12] King James Version. Holy Bible Grand Rapids: Zondervan 2001

Spiritual formation provides the Christian with the know how in worshipping God and possessing the knowledge of him as it relates to one completeness. The spiritual discipline is the practicing and exercising of that which one believes. Often times people of God become consume with tradition rather than pleasing God. The Pharisees was notorious for being concerning about the law. In addition, they practice enforcing the law but not by precepts and examples.

Chapter 3: The Process of Teaching and Learning

Since the dawning of civilization mankind has been on a spiritual journey to explore, define and understand the concept of a higher divine power or person. From the ancient ruins of the Aztecs in Central America to the remnants of a mystical past of Stonehenge in Europe, there is concrete evidence of man's constant plight to know and understand the idea of God. Who God is, what God is and even where God is. The world contains a plethora of religious systems that have been carved and evolved out of the human experience all to shed some sort of light on the idea and subject of God. This quest and exploration has become known as theology.

In order to understand theology one must first research and gain an understanding of theology and its importance. Theology is the study of God. *Theos* is the Greek word for God. Connor states "theology is the effort to intellectualize the religion, to bring to understanding and explanation the face and phases of Christianity for the purpose of teaching

Christians and evangelizing the lost"[13] (Connor, 1937). Theology offers

one the ability to explore and seek a fulfillment from within by exploring

the concept and character of God. Every individual that is created is

shaped in the image of the Creator. Because humans and or mankind is

changing and in advancing that alone proves that greater exist. We are not

mere products of biological phenomena, we are the handiwork of a divine

source. Therefore, advancement suggests that there is a constant changing

of current events and things to come. Theology can be best appreciated

through the work o through the work of the Holy Spirit as an instrument to

lead all to God through Christ his Son.

Theological task is best described as the identification or the

connecting in systematic doctrines. (Grenz, 2000)[14] Therefore, theological

task helps all to appreciate, understand and apply theology, though the

base thought of theology means one thing and the interpretation of it helps

foster a great seeking and fulfilling. Christians express their respect of

God in many forms which in return leads to a theological task at work.

---

[13] Connor, W. Christian Doctrine Nashville TN: Broad man Press (1937).

[14] Grenz, S. Theology for the community Grand Rapids, MI: Eerdmans. (2000

These individuals who believe God and chases after God expresses their desire to stay connected. Theological task is carried out through daily devotion, fellowship with other Christians in corporate worship and participation in ministerial activities and outlets. Theological task gives the opportunity for each believer to tap into the portals of fulfillment by allowing one to only achieve totality. Theology is the art and science of enjoying God through Christ in all of life. (Shaw, 2004)[15] In addition, there are four forms of noted theologies to consider: systematic; historical; biblical; and practical. Systematic theology is the summary of Christian beliefs and doctrine. Historical theology provides information from an historical point of view from an actual practical time in which we can identify from. Biblical theology gives a Bible based account of theology. Biblical theology focuses on the life, death and resurrection of Jesus Christ. Practical theology concentrates on the social issues of the church and the inner working of the ministry in which one believes the Holy Spirit as an instrument to lead all to God through Christ his Son.

---

[15] Ibid

Grenz, (Grenz, 200)[16] has three sources of theological tasks on which he proposes and discusses reasons. Scripture, culture, and interpretation are the three areas in which Grenz discusses as theological tasks. Scripture is the Word of God. It is the scripture in which we rely upon to reveal God's Word to us. Scripture is God's way of conversing with us. Culture is important in theological task because culture helps shapes individuals faith. Though we all believe in God we all comes from different cultural backgrounds. For instance, those that lives in the North verses those that lives in the South are faced with different culture experiences and background experiences. These cultural factors often play a vital role in the theological experience of the believer. Interpretation is the understanding in which an individual gathers from his or her beliefs. Scripture and culture is necessary in theological tasks but when combined interpretation is formed. An interpretation can only be gathered when present with idea and thoughts. The theological tasks Grenz[17] offers help one view theology through interpreting in a more in-depth manner. This

---

[16] Grenz, S. Theology for the community Grand Rapids, MI: Eerdmans. (2000)

[17] Grenz, S. Theology for the community Grand Rapids, MI: Eerdmans. (2000

expansive interpretation allows a more well-rounded theological perspective.

To better understand theology, theological tasks and theological motifs an individual must first gain an understanding of God through theology. There are several innate characteristics and qualities that human as living beings have. The innate qualities a human possess affords him or her the ability to know that God exist. To understand that God exist one must understand theology. Through the understanding of theology one's mind set is built and enjoys consistent expansion and development. Therefore, the living soul has the ability to allow his or her theological task to erect. Upon the erection of one's mind the theological task is derived. During this period of transformation scripture bring illumination to the mind and soul through study; while culture is being evaluated through the individual(s) eyes and an interpretation is gathered.

Therefore the true answer to the question of what theology is, is not found in the academic exploration of the subject alone but in examining the lives of those who participate in its challenging experience. To simply study God is in and of itself unfruitful and rudimentary without application to the daily life of the believer. For the theologian and the student of scripture, theology is a mere genre of academic escapades but for the Christian living his or her daily life in conventions ways while being in conventional places, theology is the application of God. The Christian learns more about the character and ways of God while constantly seeking opportunities to embracing the life changing principles and illumination that comes from theological study and discourse.

How did we get here? The ethical crisis is also a truth crisis. Significant shifts in the behaviors, beliefs, and values of Western culture have contribute to this crisis, including privatization, humanism, relativism, secularization, and pluralism. The result is the moral crisis in our nation. Leaders in government, businesses and sports are charged with various illegal and immoral acts. Church leaders are caught in unethical behaviors and activities. Our nation has lost its moral footing. Clearly, the crisis in ministerial ethics is part of a larger crisis. An examination of the effects pf privatization, humanism, relativism, secularization, and pluralism will explain how this moral crisis occurred.

Privatization in our Western world moved religion and ministry from the public to the private arena which resulted in a loss of responsibility. The inability to discuss religion in the public arena is one consequence. One religion is limited to the private arena, sharing one's faith becomes difficult and responsibility is denied. "what I do is my business". This attitude has contributed to the loss of Christian ethics both in ministry and in the pew.

Humanism teaching of ethic has not kept us with the rapid advances in our world. Our world and our churches have experienced a loss of values through humanism. In the past, the church generally taught ethics by focusing on behaviors more than values or beliefs. For an example, when my children were young, I taught them not to play between the sidewalk and the street (behavior). Later, I taught them how to distinguish safe and unsafe places and activities. (values) If I know what is wrong but not why it is wrong, I cannot make valid decisions when new options are presented.

The values shift in our society must be addressed. The private availability of immoral materials has increased. Formerly, exposure in the public arena was a deterrent to pornography and other unethical or illicit activities. In the private arena, such checks are removed. Restoring Christian ethics will demand that we clearly connect behaviors (ethics), values, and truth beliefs.

Relativism, our world and our churches have experienced a loss of truth, an erosion of the principle base through relativism. If truth is relative, there is no objective truth. If there is no objective truth, no one can say with certainty that any behavior is right or wrong. Despite the discomfort of making truth claims that prove other religions, or even other Christian religious groups, false, the church cannot afford to deny the truth. David Wells has outlined the impact on a society and its future when truth claims are lacking. The church must return to the clear pronouncement of objective truth.

Secularization, we have experienced a loss of mystery in the continuing secularization of religion. A poor spiritual focus results from a lack of spiritual training. The ultimate result is a totally secular version of Christianity, a result I fear may not be far away from some groups.

Pluralism, our churches have lost some of their identity through pluralism. In a world of relative truth, Secularization religion, lack of mystery, and loss of values, we hardly know who we are or why we exist. We have limited ability to identify ourselves as a Christian colony characterized by Christian behaviors in our effort to be Christ's disciples. The church can only lose if this truth is crisis is not addressed.

There are several internal factors that contribute to the internal.

*Lack of spiritual focus

Ministry interviews seldom ask about personal spiritual health and growth. Few ministerial training programs require spiritual-formation components. The significant requirements reflection and formation in ministerial training is the exception not the rule. Have we forgotten that spiritual leaders must be spiritual? Are we so busy pursuing God's work by methods proven in the marketplace that we have forgotten God's kingdom work is spiritual? How will unspirited people minister God's presence effectively in the church when God is barely present in their lives? Without spiritual focus, spiritual famine will come. Genuine ministry is fraught with frailty, frustration, and even failure. The greatest failure, however, may be seeking power for ministry in the physical rather than the spiritual realm.

How should ministry be measured? There are two opposite extremes. On one hand, worldly standards of success often replace spiritual evaluation. Some churches fail to appreciate effective ministry in their demand for numerical results. God's Old Testament prophets would not fared well in many modern churches.

On the other hand, some churches and ministers fail to understand the power and potential of effective ministry and suffer because of their low expectations. The ultimate measurement of ministry is faithfulness to God. Ministry that is faithful to never fails. Faithful ministry brings Gods' power to bear in this world, and God promises increase. His Word never return empty.

Worldly Expectations

Our society and churches often buy into the worldly mindset more than we like to admit. We frequently have expectations that do not appreciations that do not appreciate the elastic, flexible nature of ministry. We do not know which certainty whether ministers work for God or for churches. We affirm the former, but often practice the latter. We are more apt to clone preachers than allow valid ministry consistent with the ministers' personality.

Importance of the Theory of Free Will

An individual's environment and morals are extremely important to their development. One's obstacles and negative life experiences can greatly affect one's ability to think and rationalize appropriately. That is why it is vital for children to be loved and nurtured. They should also be given varied opportunities to make sound choices and decisions for themselves. These choices and decisions are often cultivated from their prior life experiences, knowledge and value system. Individuals are also guided by their innate sense of ethics that impinges on human decisions, and makes them feel good when they do what is right. (Laher 2011)[18] If children are deprived from this nurturing and loving environment, their life decision making process and choices may be deeply construed. C.S. Lewis states what we learn from experience depends on the kind of philosophy we bring to experience. (Lahar, 2011) Individuals are held

---

[18] Suheil, Laher. Free Will and Determinism from a Scientific and Religious Perspective. 2011

accountable and responsible for their behavior. However, we do not always determine our life circumstances. We cannot dictate what family we will be born into nor the environment that we will be reared in. Therefore, some life circumstances are beyond our control. However, we are responsible for the way that we react and respond to our positive or negative life experiences. We must choose to grow and learn from them and not use them as excuses to act or respond in a certain way/manner. One individual who used their adversity as motivation is Oprah Winfrey. Winfrey suffered from physical abuse and molestation as a child.

However, she did not seek revenge on those who mistreated her, but instead she used her adversity and experiences to grow and make a better life for herself. As a result, she became one of the most successful female television host, entrepreneur and actress. This proves that an individual can push pass their adversity and negative life experiences and succeed. So, we are ultimately still responsible and must be held accountable for our actions and choices whether those actions or choices are positive or negative. I believe that all behavioral decisions are nothing more than a reflection of our genetic and environmental history. It is imperative to have a strong moral foundation in order to make sound, solid decisions and choices. This world would be an extremely scary place to live if it was void of individuals being held accountable for their actions. Laws could therefore not be put into place or enforced for various criminal behaviors because everyone would have an excuse. In addition, individuals exercise their free will when making decisions regarding their behavior and ultimate life circumstances.

The theory of free will believes that individuals make free and independent choices without constraints. Therefore, these choices cannot be blamed on any other person or circumstance. A person's environment and upbringing cannot be considered when trying to determine why an individual made a particular choice or decision. Furthermore, an individual is responsible and should therefore be held accountable for their choices and decisions. John Fischer states that he believes that most adults are morally responsible a large majority of the time for their behavior. (Fischer, 1999) The human brain acts at both the conscious level as well as the unconscious. Therefore, consciousness makes us aware of our actions, giving us the sense that we control them. Even without this awareness, our brains can still cause our bodies to act in a certain way.

Studies have indicated and showed that consciousness is something that follows unconscious neural activity. (Zyga, 2010)[19]

Determinism threatens moral responsibility. This theory would therefore reject strong accountability and no one would be worthy to blame for their negative actions. Determinism believes that all actions, decision, and choices are the result of some type of cause and effect nature. Just because one is often aware of multiple paths and choices to make, doesn't mean one actually gets to choose one of them based on their own free will. Individual's decisions are based and driven by some uncontrollable cause that may very well result in a negative effect. This negative effect would therefore be justified and blameless. So, how would society/government handle legitimate procedures for wrong doing? Our resources for consequences due to criminal behavior would be limited. In these cases, rejection of strong accountability would prove to be at a disadvantage. We would therefore not have any justification of criminal punishment. Moreover, individuals must be accountable for their actions in order to ensure a safe society in which we live. Currently, in order to be found

----

[19] Lisa, Zyga. (2010) Free Will is an Illusion. PhysOrg .Retrieved from PhysOrg.com

guilty, a criminal must be considered responsible for his or her actions; otherwise, a criminal can be found not guilty by reason of insanity. Regardless of an individual's societal affiliation ambition, avarice, self-love, vanity, friendship, generosity, and public spirit are the source of all actions among mankind. (Hume) Humans draw from their past experiences and inferences concerning their future endeavors. It is evident that we turn to our prior knowledge and experiences to assist us in making decisions regarding our future decisions. According to the determinism theory, we are habit of our past and environment. Therefore, each one of those aspects shapes our behaviors and decisions. All events in life including our moral choices are completely shaped by previous existing causes. Many deterministic views support that we are merely conscious beings, solely being controlled by a combination of our chemistry and external environmental forces. The human brain has the ability to acts at a conscious as well as an unconscious state.

Consciousness makes individuals aware of their actions. But even without this awareness, our brains can still induce our bodies to act. Studies have indicated and showed that consciousness is something that follows unconscious neural activity. (Zyga, 2010)[20] Because individuals are often aware of multiple paths to take, that doesn't mean that they will actually get to choose one of them based on their own free will. Their free will is often impaired by their prior life experiences and environments. The psychological ramifications therefore tend to lean toward the determinism theory. However, law and order must be maintained within all societies; therefore, individuals must be responsible and held accountable for their actions even if biological or genetic factors were involved or present. In order to maintain order, the free will theory must be adhered to and followed through. So, one must contend to not allow these factors to drive their decision-making process.

Even though individuals are not biologically responsible for their actions according to the deterministic theory, in order to minimize criminal activity, people should still be held accountable, and be punished when necessary. This punishment will help ensure a safe as well as organized society. We cannot continue to make excuses for our actions. Psychiatrists and other experts on human behavior should therefore not be involved in initial judicial court proceedings. The jury should simply

---

[20] Lisa, Zyga. (2010) Free Will is an Illusion. PhysOrg .Retrieved from PhysOrg.com

determine and be held accountable for whether or not a defendant is guilty of committing a crime. Jurors should not be assigned the task of determining a defendant's mental status at the time of criminal activities.

Consequently, if the defendant is found guilty, a court-appointed panel of experts should advise on the most appropriate punishment and treatment for the defendant. However, determinism should not be an excuse or reason to prevent appropriate punishment for criminal behavior. Individuals still must be held accountable and responsible for all of their actions and decisions. We all must strive to overcome and learn from our varied backgrounds and life experiences. The deterministic theory refutes the belief that all individuals must be held accountable for their own actions no matter what their prior experiences, genetic makeup or environments may have entailed. These factors should be considered but not obstruct the fact that we as individuals must yet and still be held accountable and responsible for making the ultimate decisions in our lives.

Importance of Theory of Consciousness and Unconsciousness

An Individual's environment and morals are extremely important to their development. One's obstacles and experiences can greatly affect one's ability to rationalize appropriately and make effective decisions. That is why it is vital for children to be loved and nurtured. They should also be given various opportunities to make sound choices and decisions for themselves throughout childhood. These choices and decisions are often cultivated from their prior life experiences, knowledge and value system. If children are deprived from this nurturing and loving environment, their life decision making process and choices may be deeply construed. C. S. Lewis states that we learn from experience depend on the kind of philosophy we bring to experience (Lahar, 2011)[21]. I believe that many behavioral decisions are nothing more than a reflection of our genetic and environmental history. So, it is imperative to have a strong moral foundation in order to make sound, solid, decisions and choices. Therefore, I strongly believe that most individuals utilize the unconscious process as well as the conscious thought process to assist them in the decision making. Conscious thought cannot take place without unconscious process also being activated as well. Conscious thought however is highly constrained by a low capacity of consciousness. In

---

[21] Suheil, Laher. Free Will and Determinism from a Scientific and Religious Perspective. 2011

addition, conscious thought is thought that requires attention. The human brain acts at both the conscious level as well as the unconscious. Therefore, consciousness makes us aware of our actions, giving us the sense that we control them.

Memories and perceptions can greatly influence one's decision making process. Unconsciousness may be entirely composed of ideas that were previously conscious and have been repressed. (De Sousa, 2011)[22] I strongly believe that most individuals are creatures of habit. Therefore, it is extremely important to form and utilize positive and constructive habits. We often draw from these positive or negative habits consciously or unconsciously. Moreover, I believe these habits that are formed greatly affect and influence the various decisions that we make in life. In addition, an individual's positive or negative memories can impact their decision-making process and their perception of various situations. Individuals often draw from and make decisions based on their prior experience of the issue at hand. These experiences are based on short cuts known as heuristics that influence as well as impact one's decision making practices.

---

[22] De Sousa, Avinash, Fruedian Theory and Conscoiusness: A Conceptual Analysis, Mens Sana Monographs, Vol. 9(1), Jan-Dec 2011

These rules of thumb and strategies link prior experiences and situations to current ones.

The task of thinking can be delegated to the unconscious processes. This unconscious thought can be defined and referred to object-relevant or task-relevant cognitive or affective thought processes that occur while conscious attention is directed elsewhere. (Dijksterhuis & Nordgren, 2006)[23] The unconscious thought principle consists of the conscious and unconscious. Attention is the key component to distinguish the difference between unconscious thought and conscious thought. However, conscious thought cannot exist without unconscious processes existing at the same time. Conscious capacity is limited and cannot multi task. Therefore, consciousness cannot do more than one objective at a time. Unconscious thought has a high capacity; therefore, unconscious thought has greater organization of information in memory. Moreover, unconscious thinkers seem to make better decisions and choices. These thinkers think critically beyond the surface. Unconscious thinkers have

---

[23] AP Dijksterhuis and Loran Nordgren, A Theory of Unconscious Thought, Social Association for Psychological Science Vol 1 (2), 2006

been found to think more creatively and outside of the box. Quality decisions are made when utilizing unconscious thought processes that are free of complex problems. It is imperative that the unconscious thought have access to important and factual information that is free of faulty experiences and recollections. Intuitions are the summary judgments the unconscious provides when it is ready to decide. (Dijksterhuis & Nordgren, 2006)[24]

The vital core function that anchors the behavioral repertoire of every organism that has a brain is the unconscious processes. Primitive organisms are tremendously controlled by unconscious processes. Unconscious operations take place in the brain automatically, without the intervention or review or a central, integrated self;(Viamontes & Beitman, 2000)[25] Imaging studies have shown that if the brain is awake, at rest, or attending to other external task, the awake brain still shows comparable levels of energy usage. External sensory stimuli are not received or interpreted in a small space; however, they are experienced and seen when

---

[24] Ibid

[25] Viamontes& Beitman, 2000

subjective personal context is maintained without conscious effort through all of our waking hours, in a specialized manner, when we dream. (Viamontes& Beitman, 2000)[26] Unconscious circuits are able to produce information and responses more rapidly than the conscious perception. Many daily functions that are vital for survival are controlled and managed by unconscious circuits. These unconscious circuits have access to many possible responses such as modulatory neurotransmitter and hormone release, activation of genetically encoded behavioral sequences, modulation of atomic tone, and activation of learned behavioral sequences. In addition, unconscious processes are continuously receiving sensory information and predicting its meaning of innate and learned pattern. The unconscious process prepares the body to handle the current situation at hand and has been predicted. An important function of the unconscious processes is the activation of learned motor sequences. This function is a frequent factor and contributor to psychopathology. It is important to learn appropriate and acceptable ways of making effective decisions because once an action sequence has been learned through the conscious mechanisms; it can be controlled by the unconscious. So

---

[26] ibid

learning how to drive a car correctly or learning rules to a particular sport can be controlled by the unconscious. Therefore, it is essential to that these learned action sequences are correct and not faulty or wrong. Physical violence is also another good example of these learned action sequences. Consequently, individuals that are violent may have a genetic predisposition for their behavior or they could have also experienced some violent behavior in childhood. This violent behavior experiences could activate or trigger internal representations of violence via mirror neurons.

Determinism believes that all actions, decisions, and choices are the result of some type of cause and effect nature. Just because one is often aware of multiple paths and choices to make, does not mean one actually gets to choose one of them based on their own free will. Individual's decisions are based and driven by some uncontrollable cause that may well result in a negative result. So faulty or negative experiences can hinder positive decision making processes. According to the deterministic theory, we are habit of our past and environment. Therefore, each one of those aspects shapes our behaviors and decision making process. All events in life including our moral choices are complexly shaped by previous existing causes. Many deterministic views support that we are merely conscious beings, solely being controlled by a combination of our chemistry and external environmental forces. Determinism threatens moral responsibility. This theory would therefore reject strong accountability and no one would be worthy of blame of their negative actions. The human brain has the ability to act at a conscious as well as an unconscious level. Because individuals are often aware of multiple paths to take, that does not mean that they will actually going to choose one of them based on their own free will. Their free will is often times impaired by prior life experiences and environments. Therefore, these prior experiences and memories are retrieved and often referred to in order to make current daily decisions.

Daily decision making is a part of everyday life. What shirt should I wear? What will I eat for breakfast? Should I go to the school basketball game or football game? Therefore, the daily decision making process cannot be avoided. However, life also dictates making more important and complex decisions. When it is necessary to make those types of decisions, it is often necessary that we pull from our vast knowledge and life experiences. Unfortunately, these life experiences may not always be positive and productive. However, our decisions and choices should be. These decisions and choices can become deeply construed if our memories are faulty and of negative effect. Moreover, it is vital that our environments produce positive experiences and opportunities to grow and learn. Unfortunately, these positive conducive environments are not always obtainable; therefore, our unconscious reflects on these negative experiences to help in current situations that we face in life. Unfortunately, these negative experiences can produce both positive or negative decision making results and processes. Even when individuals drive to make conscious decisions those decisions can easily be influenced by the unconscious processes to retrieve prior knowledge and remembrance of negative outcomes. Therefore, these negative outcomes and experiences tend to control the current decision making process. It is important to push past those repressed memories to live and produce healthy decision making processes.

Suggestions for Recovering Ethical Ministry

Finding a solution to the crisis in ministerial ethics will not be easy. No panacea exists. Encouraging ethical ministry requires focus in two areas-ministers and ministry. How can we develop ethical ministers and ministries? To begin, we must recognize that ethics is not only a minster issues, but also is a church issues. Churches build ministers as much as ministers build churches. Churches shape ministers and ministry by their expectations and demands. Church must believe in powerful ministry. Ministers must develop purposeful ministries.

We will not restore ethics in ministry until we understand the reasons for its loss. Ethics sits at the top of the principle-values-ethics pyramid. Our worldview (principle base) informs and supports our values that in turn determine our behaviors. A person's worldview is the assumptions one makes about the universe and how it operates. The foundation of ethics is one's belief system. Changes in worldview of our society quickly or reverse the slide into relativity.

Thus the question is asked how ministers and ministry must change and how the required change can be accomplished. Restoring ethics in ministry demands clear belief systems for ministers and churches, and the identification and reaffirmation of Christian values. We must learn to think like Christ to develop Christian values and behaviors.

The Minister

First, we must provide better training for ministers. The church must demand adequately prepared ministers. The church must demand adequately prepared ministers. What is an adequate ministerial training model for producing capable, competent ministers? While it is true that every Christian can serve, and many can stand and talk before a class, ministry demands more. This responsibility of ministry is three-fold keeping our promises, honoring our commitments, and maintaining moral lifestyles. A step toward these responsibility is the inclusion of ethic in ministerial training models. Our ministry training schools must teach that ministry is principle and values. We must demand training that addresses the personal spiritual attitudes and learn how to live by Christian worldview that defines and training for thinking like Christ; and connects beliefs, values, and ethics. Minister must emerge from their training with a strong commitment to personal spirituality, blameless character, and morality above reproach.

Second, we must hold ministers accountable for ministry. Ministry does not always produce the desired results, but ministers should be accountable for their lives, studies and ministry activities. We must encourage a greater openness in those who ministers, and willingness in the church to let them be human, confess weaknesses, and receive loving support from the church.

Finally, ethical ministry requires ministers committed to ministry, who know that the rewards as the world measures success may be few, but that the job is worth doing and can be done. Only when I believe in what I am doing can I find the strength to develop the mind of Christ and to live by the principles and values of Christ.

The Church

Churches must commit developing better support for ministry and better understanding of ministers. Churches build ministers more that ministers build churches. The church's interest in ethical ministry extends to every Christian servant. What steps should the church take to help recover ethical ministry?

- *First,* the church must demand the integration of principles, values, and ethics in the lives of those who minister. Ethics is concrete; every Christian is responsible for character.

- *Second,* the church should focus on and demand accountability for the task of ministry rather that the results. Churches must be prepared to support ministry and to help set reasonable expectations for accomplishment.

- *Third,* churches must strive to develop an open atmosphere that encourages honesty and vulnerability among all Christians, including those who minster, allowing all to be human. Ethical ministry demands that members and ministers go into the world guided by Christian ethics.

- *Fourth,* we must develop better support systems within the church for those who minister.

- *Five,* churches must develop a better understand of ministry. Each year preach at least one sermon on the nature of ministry.

The church needs to understand ministry and to understand your ministry. You are accountable to them; they are your support system.

- *Sixth,* the church must develop a fellowship that allows the minister to become an authentic part of the local congregation.

- *Finally,* the church must be ethical in its treatment of ministers, members, one another, and the world.

These simple steps will not solve every problem, but they can start the church down the road to restored confidence in ministry. Ministers will live better, preach and teach better. Ministers' families will benenfit. Ministers will find support based from church leaders, a better understanding of their role, and will be better able to meet the challenges of their congregation. The church will enjoy better teaching and preaching. The church will benefit from powerful ministries that touch lives. Finally, the world will be encouraged by ethical ministry to believe in Jesus.

When ministers believe in themselves and churches believe in ministry, the result will be a world that believes in Christ.

A church on the move is a church that seeks to grow and soar. With the proper guidance the church and or organization will excel. The leader and or pastor are skilled at understanding the proper use of technology that can enhance the office management, organization of ministries, fiscal operations, collections of tithes and offerings and most importantly the worship experience. A thriving, dynamic church must have vision and be insightful. Teamwork is what capable administration is all about. A good leader and or pastor divide objectives for all manageable parts and assign them appropriately, anticipate problems. The pastor must have foresight which will dissolve conflicts when they arrive.

According to researchers, the pastor's (leader) roles should include but not be limited to the following: How does the denomination, local/state/ regional/national staff feel about the ministry of this church? What is the potential growth? What are the skills needed to develop the church potential? What is the history of the ministry of the church? Where are they now? What will be the cost of relocation? Who will assume costs? What will be the salary? Though the pastor understands his call he must be very sure not to not curse darkness. The church is a spiritual entity. Though strategic systems is evident in today's thriving ministries monies must be brought into proper prospective. Tithing is how the Bible encourages members to support their local ministry. The Bible, which is God's holy word encourages and admonitions believers to give of their time, talent, and treasure. (Genesis 28: 22, Leviticus 27:30-32, Malachi 3:8-10 and Matthew 23:23)[27] To better understand strategic systems Church Corporation must be implied. First, area to consider is corporation sole. Corporation sole is led by one individual who cannot be usurped. An example of corporation sole is the Roman Catholic Church bishop. Another area of concern is Trustee Corporation which where states grant power is given to persons on behalf of the congregation. Once such persons are elected in trustee corporation full control of church property or entrusted to their care. Membership Corporations is easier understood; it is comprised of the entire congregation no distinction between trustees and society. However, it said that membership is similar to that of a civil or business corporation. The variety of power of the strategic systems help

---

[27] King James Version. Holy Bible Grand Rapids: Zondervan 2001

builds and establishes the church for growth in a productive but progressive society.

In my research and studies, I have found that the church and the churches I am familiar have a strategic system. I am saddened to report you and the class that often times the plan is not implemented. Those whom established the organization for the church was led of God; therefore being led of God all things needed was established at its beginning to be successful. However, we as the church allow personnel whom should not be elected hold key positions. Though many possess knowledge of some form of business does not mean one's knowledge of business is for the church arena. Strategic systems can be best described as understanding the goal and implementing ways to achieve the said mission collective. However the strategically all persons involved must have a firm knowledge of how to obtain and a willingness to obtain. These systems can be and are successful and effective if placed in the proper hands. First and most importantly the leader must be a go getter. If the chairman does not have a firm grasp and concern which involves involvement then the church and organization will fail. As a pastor there are certain strategic concerns I would have and I would implement. It is my belief that all pastors are system persons. If no form of system is put in place within the ministry then the ministry will not survive. Bylaws, constitutions and goals are all forms of system that the organization must adhere too. Although the church is not a business again some form of business and systems will be put in play for all the ministries created within will function. The Pastor is the chairman of the church's business; all outreaches of all sorts must be overseen. My biggest concern as Senior Pastor would be implementing ministries such as: Christian Education; evangelism; clothes closest for needy. In addition, a skill bank will be used to access all the abilities of all members and to ensure every person has a place in the ministry. Therefore, no Christian will be left behind because his or her skill will be placed properly within the ministry. Every great leader especially a pastor must understand business and spirituality. First, I will prayer for God's leading spiritually and secular. I will have persons employed who understand the secular side of business. In addition, they will be persons who can and will be spiritually led. This will ensure for a successful business in strategic systems and church development. Each and every member will have a place in the ministry to allow his or her gift to flourish. By allowing all members to function in their calling will progress the ministry. Once abilities have been access of all persons everyone will be placed in their proper place.

As a Senior Pastor spiritually, I will equip my church by allowing the ministry listed in Ephesians 4:11-16[28] to flow. These gifts have been given to church by God himself to perfect the saint and the ministry. God has made known a message for His people that will met all particular needs. These gifts help the saints for the working of the ministry. Those who are in pastoral positions must care for God's people. Spiritual gifts are given to the church to perfect the saints and for the edifying of the body of Christ.

As a called leader commissioned to do the work of God, one must be sensitivity to the voice of God. First, a believer must have a keen ear to hear and know the voice of God. Along with a keen ear and believer needs a pure heart. The ensuring of a pure heart while listening to God allows ones to become a better you in the midst of God speaking. Another interesting factor to consider is the removal of all clutter. Clutter consists

---

[28] King James Version. Holy Bible Grand Rapids: Zondervan 2001

of anything in one life that will become a stumbling block for an onward Christian soldier. The allowance of clutters leads to traps, snares and hindrances. Understanding how to hear God includes tuning into the right channels. The proper channels include knowing God's voice by His approach; knowing God's voice by His Word and its contents therein; and lastly by the results it produces. There are signals in which we must have or develop in order to ensure we are in right standing to hear from God. The mindset of a believer must be first the mind of God. After desiring and walking after the mind of Christ is when the gifts God has design will be deployed. In addition, I can honestly admit that faith is related more to the concept of national self-determination and identity to in one's faith.

Thinking of religion, I realized that spirituality is not the only part of my national self-identity, but faith is also integrated in the concept of being Christian; thus Christianity relates history to present and allows stability to recess in the lives of others. Therefore, in my conclusion, pastors uses strategic systems and must implement programs within the local church to help assist all persons who desires to excel within his or her spirituality.

For centuries theologians have offered to the world around them an insight into their world of study and revelation. The commentary that is presented from their life long journey in the truths of scripture and spiritual thought has impacted the lives of every believer across the world. Though the foundation of the truths expressed in their writings are uniformly premised on key Christian doctrine, the variance of their positions presents perspectives and reasoning that are both unique and at times complementary to each other. Their revelation and theological perspective is shaped not only by the acquired knowledge and skill in the scriptures but most importantly through the life experiences that have formulated their world view.

In the article, "Hume Versus Kant: Faith, Reason and Feelings" John Milbank focuses on many different concept of faith and reasoning. However, an area to consider is transcendental. Transcendental encompasses the intellectual so of mankind. Therefore philosophy is built and establishes to help determines the mind set of an individual. The ability to reason and or to make an assumption is another area to focus upon when understanding transcendental foundations. Kant came to the realization that "reason has to make certain assumptions and trust in the reasonableness of the real." Kant understands the power of faith and its effectiveness. Hume unlike Kant try to explore the human's mind through experimental study leaving no place for faith but leaving everything to reason. Hume believed that human thinking arrived by his or her own doing.

John Polkinghorne the author of "Scripture and an Evolving Creation" gives an interesting exegesis on scripture as it pertains to creation. All Christian believers understand that the world and all therein was and is created by God. Not anything that is made and was made was created outside of God. Genesis gives the account of creation of all living things and how it was created. Polkinghorne defines the ideas of creationism and evolution. Creationism and evolution has not root or no ground; before living things can evolve from itself then the very thing it evolved from must have an organ. An area in which Mr. Polkinghorne focuses is self-consciousness. His perspective of self-consciousness proves that we have an origin before creation. Therefore humans received their innate ability to reason from their creator God. Though evolution teachings challenges cosmic and terrestrials aspects one can see how great God is and humans still in awe of His powerful and majestic creations.

In the article Starting Point, Pope Benedict XVI shares his thoughts of teaching of Jesus teaching of love your enemies. Because we live in a world that desires to please itself; the disciples of Jesus are often challenged. Jesus understood and yet He understands the hardships his followers must endure. Pope Benedict XVI urges the world and those of the Catholic faith to love in spite of their current statuses whether it is oppression or depression. Some have been known to oppress and depress others. If and when one feels he or she is placed in such a dilemma one must exercise the love of Christ. If when one gives the best of their service telling the word that the Savior has come, do not be dismayed. For God will understand and say well done thou good and faithful servant. We Christians demonstrate love God then sees His Son Jesus. Therefore, the Christian is infused with more power from God to stand and extend His love aboard.

Considering the three theologians who are listed - Pope Benedict XVI; John Polkinghorne; and John Milbank and their revelation and perspective it is clearly evident that which is both similar and contrasting. The true beauty of this revelatory diversity is the idea that each theologian can find his or her own place within the heart and mind of an individual somewhere across our global community. As we examine their commentary, produced by hours of study and inner meditation, we began to participate in the theological process by formulating our own unique theologies and understanding of the who, how, when, where and why of God. Just like all theologians we share our understanding and perspective of God with the world around us. We share it through our daily witness and lifestyle. We share our theology through our participation in corporate worship, prayer and common fellowship with other believers. We also share our theology with future generations as we raise our children, molding and shaping their little minds into what we believe is proper, right and good. The key factor in appreciating theologians and their respective Revelation is to center our focus not to what is so different about each doctrine presented, but to identify the commonality between them all and be open minded to allowing the Holy Spirit to illuminate our own hearts and minds to build and establish truth for and within ourselves.

Since the dawn of civilization men have experienced life, pondered its philosophical attributes and conveyed the results of such ponderings to others. Thus is the creation of a popular thing called, perspective – the stance or opinion that one holds on any particular subject as a result of their respective experiences. With man's awareness of the concept of God, mankind has developed a perspective and opinion concerning God and other spiritual concepts. As with all opinions and perspectives, everyone has one and sometimes they are slightly off based. Though our perspectives are subject to numerous fallacies we yet tend to hold them in high regard as being right and true, near print worthy in a sense. Thus, the concept of our personal perspective as being a "book" is established.

The "two books" reflects upon the Holy Scripture and one's personal walk or theological perspective. When considering the two books theory one must look deep within. The Holy Bible (the Canon) is the primary authority for all things pertains to life. In addition, the Holy Scripture is a guideline to daily living; in which one is provide the opportunity to know God's instructions. The Canons' purpose is to enrich the lives of believers in to righteousness. Theological perspective is gained from one's every day interaction and knowledge of God. One's theological perspective is exercised from his or her theological expression of God. The Bible is the basis for living a holy and separated life unto God as well as God communicating to man. Therefore, the "two books" are a combination of man's perspective and outlet in keeping in touch with Almighty God.

Many theologians have discussed the idea and perspective of knowing God through revelation. Theologians believe that spiritual thought is undergoing by every human; however it is what the individual(s) do concerning their thought. In addition, the commentaries researches indicate revelation and theological expression is knowledge found in scriptures. Revelation is God's revealed plan to man. In order to experience a revelation one must have his or her self in a place to hear and receive. To properly apply a revelation two concepts of consideration must be adhere to approaching and interpreting. How one approaches his or her revelation determines their growth in God. An individual approach is determined by their submission to the voice and will of God. If any man be in Christ let him first deny himself, then pick up his cross and follow after Christ. The interpreting approach is important it gives one the opportunity to interpret what is being revealed. Many times people and or persons can become confuse if he or she misinterprets what has been revealed. The confusion or the misinterpretation can be combated if one studies his or her Bible. Still He speaks from eternity. Those whom have a futuristic viewpoint takes the scripture literal. When one takes on this viewpoint he or she are able to accept the revealing plan of God. J.I. Packer, a theologian, states human relationships that grow must have five elements: accepting, asking, promising, pleasing, and when necessary apologizing. (Packer 1994)[29] Therefore, followers of Christ are able to have access to God through revelation when are Christ atoned. (2 Peter 1:4)[30] In addition, Christians must have a communion with God regularly. Communing with God the Creator is a personal relationship that one needs to help determine one' Revelation. Theologian John Polkinghorne focuses and taught on self-consciousness. Theologian Polkinghorne concentrated on the idea one must dig from within to become and or to make better. Mediating upon the though Polkinghorne present leads one to know that general revelation is at work here. Polkinghorne reflects upon general

---

[29] PACKER, J.I. (1994). Knowing God
[30] King James Version. Holy Bible Grand Rapids: Zondervan 2001

revelation considering the idea of one working toward a goal through every day practices with a conscious mindset. Pope Benedict XVI, in the article "Starting Point" encouraged believers and follower of the Catholic faith to love your enemies like you do yourself. This modern theologian is teaching love beyond conditions. Loving without conditions allows one to exercise special and general Revelation. When one love without conditions he or she takes on the mindset of God. To love those that hurt you takes a special anointing. In addition, loving without regards leaves one to expresses the undying love Jesus Christ in doing so special revelation will be revealed due to this type of love. Another present day theologian is John Milbank. Theologian John Milbank is noted for reasoning and faith which represent general revelation. Reasoning and faith incorporates ones innate ability to take general knowledge and make the best decisions given. Faith becomes a factor when an individual believes in his or her self when faced with decision making and advancing in day to day activities.

The intertwining role of special revelation (Scripture) and general revelation in the theological task of discovering God requires commitment and dedication. Special Revelation only comes when one is attentive to the workings of the Holy Spirit. There are things God shares with only His children. Each time God shares and imparts within men it is a special revelation. The determining factors in special Revelation are God's choice to reveal (show) to an individual(s). It is no goodness of one's own that makes him or her worthy to be chosen for special Revelation. Special Revelation are not only for oneself but for the greater good of all persons. General revelation comes from every day interaction throughout life; there's nothing special about common practices. Special Revelation comes into play when something occurs outside the everyday norm of revelation. God has infused himself in all human beings; therefore for God to speak to man's inner spirit is no problem. Special Revelation are an unveiling truths. Men must study the Word of God constantly and steadfastly. In order to interpret Revelation properly, one must know the Holy Scriptures. It is essential that a clear understanding of scripture provides a true since of Revelation. Though some would think that visions of insight are haphazard they are one form of revelation to man.

General Revelation and special Revelation reveal the plans of God for the lives of human beings and all must be grateful to His undying loving. It is God who gives all contents pertaining to life to His children through His chosen aspect of Revelation. Those whom adhere to the Revelation given lives blessed and fulfilled lives. The greatest attributes of God are revealed to man though limitations do exist within human language. It is evident that God desire is to bring man back to His original plan, redemption. As we go through our Christian walk we will always have the comparison of theological perspectives and more especially the contrast between our view and the viewpoint of the scripture. We must always ensure that our developing theologies align themselves with the truths of God's word. We are living in a day that is full of heresies, fallacies and false doctrine and it imperative that striving the more for orthodoxy in our theological perspective and approach.

Chapter Four: Commissioned with Resources from Christ

The Intertestamental period is known as "Four Hundred Silent Years." It is understood that during this moment in history God's voice was not heard through the prophets. Although, the voice of God was not heard numerous change of events indeed took place. The Intertestamental period reflect back up the Old Testament scripture leading into the developmental phase of the New Testament era and the appearance of Christ. There are new concepts and or ideas that develop in between the Old and New Testaments.

The Historical background to the New Testament is centered on the Jewish concepts. The Jews was very instrumental during this age of silence from heaven. The Persian period includes a Jewish state overtaken by Nebuchadnezzar men. These Babylonians destroyed Jerusalem and enslaved many. The Jews went under Persian influence when Babylon was overtaken by Persia and her allies. The Greek period (influence) came into perspective when Alexander the great rose to power and lead his men to conquerors. Alexander the great, the victories allow him and his forces to become world dominating for that period. Because the Jews did not challenge Alexander the great, intern he treated them well. The Ptolemaic

dynasty influence controlled the Jews for a century. During the rule of the

Ptolemaic dynasty the Jews had good living. Some commentators believe

the Jews were very prosperous. In addition, the Septuagint was produce

under this dynasty rule. The Seleucids took control however; much to

the Seleucids surprise the Jews was devoted to Gods' law. There again the

Jews had taken on another way of the pagan nation. The Jews was

introduced to a newer form of idolatry. Finally, the Hasmonean period

here the Jews are in the hands of power struggle leader and or group.

Although, power struggling was a problem, the Jewish religious life was

replenished. Though the Jews experienced many leaders and groups

overtaken them; the people of God still had a mind toward the things of

God. One can conclude that God still hand is hands on His people, even in

the midst of transition.

In addition to the Jewish historical background warriors and

leaders such as "Maccabeus" is taking note of. Maccabeus succeeds his

father in leading upon his father, Matthias death. In the book of

"Maccabeus" it is recorded of his detailed victory. Maccabeus, the hammer, was successful in rebelling especially using guerilla warfare tactics. Maccabeus was so successful in guerilla warfare until it made him nearly impossible to defeat. This young leader is noteworthy because in 143 B.C. peace was achieved and the Jews became an independent state.

According to Saint John 4: 25[31] a dilemma arose among the people of God; the religious leaders of that day had a difficult time accepting Jesus and his teachings. The Jews and Samaritans all was oppressed by the religious leaders of that day. All knew that Law. All had heard that a Messiah would could. The people misunderstood how the Lord (the Messiah) would come. Because the religious leaders were oppressing the people desire a Messiah would come and over taken the Roman government. The people desire a King and or Lord with an iron fist. "The woman saith unto him, I know that Messia cometh to which I called Christ.........he will tell us all things St. John 4: 25."[32] Because the Lord came as a lowly servant but with the power and the authority as God they could not receive. There were difficulties in receiving because he did not demonstrate the characteristics of one whom will destroy all and give the

---

[31] King James Version. Holy Bible Grand Rapids: Zondervan 2001
[32] ibid

people their desired victory. Yet, God still had His hand not only on His people but on all people. For all mankind has been created in the likeness and image of God.

The early Christians and the church had practical issues that Apostle Paul addressed. In the Pauline Epistles, Paul addressed the church at Corinth and the issues this young reformation faced. The Apostle Paul's dedication to the believers at Corinthian is a good depiction of an overseer's care and concern. The purpose for Corinthian epistle encompasses sanctification and reconciliation. Sanctification is being set a part. Reconciliation is to remove enmity between individuals or parties. Man must be reconciled back to God through sanctification. The apostle's writing of I Corinthians is, first to prove instructions on how to handle severe problems in the church and second, to provide doctrinal clarity for new converts. The recordings of II Corinthians were written to reestablish authority and to establish order for preservation of the church.

Corinth was a city known for its corruption. Living in Corinth offered a life of luxury. To better understand this wealthy city is to understand Roman rule which in encompasses sexual immortality. In addition, he references Jesus Christ as being the head of the church. Then, Paul encourages all to be in fellowship. (I Cor. 1:9)[33] As the apostle continues to write he empowers and establishes sound doctrine for believers to adhere too. Paul was well aware that the Corinthian believers were spiritual gifted and talented. He reminds them while they are awaiting the Lord's return believers must remain proactive until Jesus comes.

The Corinthian Church still faced issues during the writings of II Corinthians. (Benware 2003 p.185) The Apostle Paul appointed Titus to go assist at Corinth. (II Corinthians 2: 12-13)[34] Paul reaffirmed the Corinthian church that the ultimate authority in the church is Jesus Christ the Lord. The troubles arising in the church had to be controlled. The Corinthian saints were reminded of giving to the poor and needy in Judea and repentance. A genuine passion for the gospel ministry is what the apostle preached. As Paul seeks to provide in-depth understanding to the church he addresses the following areas: teachings about true ministry, exhortations, instructions about giving, and the apostolic ministry.

---

[33] King James Version. Holy Bible Grand Rapids: Zondervan 2001
[34] ibid

The doctrine taught by the apostle targeted specific areas of concern as they relate to what Jesus taught. Paul pinpointed the manner an individual responds to the Word of God. If a believer fails to live upright he or she will become an undeveloped Christian spiritually. A believer must allow the Word of God to become alive in him. (I Cor. 2:14-3:4)[35] Knowledge appropriation gives an individual spiritual development where they can grow productively. Jesus taught that "Man cannot live by bread alone but by every word that proceed out of the mouth of God." (Matt. 4:4)[36] The apostle Paul reminded believers the knowledge of God is the cross of Christ. Therefore an individual can only see his need for Christ when he views the cross of Calvary. This is the message Christ preached and taught as he walked among men. Hebrews 9:22[37].....Without the shedding of blood there is no remission of sin.

Christian theology can be gathered from Paul's teachings. First, he offered the believer in instructions on morals and discipline. (I Cor. 5:1-

---

[35] King James Version. Holy Bible Grand Rapids: Zondervan 2001
[36] Ibid

[37] Ibid

3)[38] Second, he addresses immorality in the church and how it should not be. (I Cor. 6:12-20)[39]. His next area of concern is the problems of those in ministry; matters of marriage (I Cor.7:1-40)[40]; matters of doubtful things (I Cor.8:1-11:1)[41]; matters of worship and ministry (I Cor. 11-2-14:40[42]) and the matter of resurrection (I Cor. 15:1-58) finally, the personal suffering required of a child of God. The Christian theology as the apostle taught informs the believers as to his sacrifices of pleasure and gain. In addition, the apostle final thought was repent and turn away from sin.

The writing of this Corinthian letter was written during a turmoil and conflict with some individuals within the Corinthian church. However, the Apostle Paul expresses deep passion within this epistle to encourage wholeness. Paul's heartfelt emotions are moved due to all the conflict the church experiences. At the same time, joy is felt by the apostle his desire was not for himself but for God's glory in him through Jesus

---

[38] ibid
[39] ibid
[40] ibid
[41] King James Version. Holy Bible Grand Rapids: Zondervan 2001
[42] ibid

Christ. It is interesting to note that the Apostle Paul wrote this to the Romans from Corinth. His writings were not for the Corinthians, the Jews and the Greeks along but for all follower of Christ the Lord. Because of the depravity of man the apostle saw the need to write and build the ministry.

The apostolic authority in which the Apostle Paul exercise shows a leader whom cares and who encourages. The apostle is a representative of the Lord Jesus. However, he receives no credit and seeks no recognition. It is the genuine love the apostle demonstrates that allows all to see the love of God disbursed abroad. The churches in Corinth was not established and left unattended but overseen by its founder.

Gentile Conversion

The Gentiles Conversion comprise a group of people whom were not the majority but the minority, however, they too are included in the Master's plan. There are occasions where Jesus involved the Gentiles in His ministry. In addition, scripture shows that Jesus performed miracles in Gentile regions. The Gentiles are noted in Acts 22:3-21. The Apostle Paul will be instrumental in reaching and teaching the Gentile nations.

Paul will become an important factor in the Gentiles conversion. The Lord soon revealed to Paul His plan for the Gentiles and the journey he would have to take. Paul travel extensively creating a busy timeline of events. The apostle's timeline of journeys would include a mission trip in A.D. 47 (Acts 13 and 14); then another journey in A.D. 50 (Acts 15 and 18); finally his last journey before imprisonment was A.D. 53 (Acts 15 and 21). Paul's effectiveness in ministry lead to an explosive impact on the gospel message being shared abroad and the Gentiles being converted, therefore the Gentiles conversion was imperative.

An important change of events occurred to the church. The church is now introduced to and begins outreach in the area of evangelism. Although, the church has been established, evangelism will ensure the church's longevity. Evangelism is a vital part of the church's mission act of offering or inviting one to be part of greater. In order for the gospel to reach the utmost parts of the earth missionaries are needed and selected. Paul and Barnabas are chosen, Paul selected as the leader of the pact. The Apostle Paul took many journeys as a missionary with his companions. He is noted for taking three major missionary journeys that impacted the church's growth and development. The first missionary journey began with Paul journey to the island of Cyprus. (Acts 13:1-28:31)[43] Then, the missionary sailed to Asia Minor which includes Antioch, Lystra and Derbe. In each city missionaries evangelized and established churches. On the second missionary journey, Paul and his companions went and overseen the newly established churches from the first missionary journey. (Acts 15:36-18:22)[44] During Paul second missionary journey he shifted his attention directly to the Gentiles ensuring his preaching and teaching was received. After reaffirming the newly established churches Paul continued on his third missionary. He entered regions of Galatia; Phrygia followed by Ephesus and taught there for 3 years. (Acts 18:23-21:16)[45] Paul's journey was deterred for a while at Troas; due to hardships.

The apostle had been warned to be aware of those whom sought after him and was imprisoned for 4 years due to the preaching of the gospel. Roman authorities and Jewish leaders despised him just as they did

---

[43] King James Version. Holy Bible Grand Rapids: Zondervan 2001
[44] ibid
[45] ibid

our Lord. (Acts 21:17-28:31)[46] Paul was carried from Jerusalem to Caesarea and Rome. Each place Paul was taken he was tired and persecuted. He soon then requested to be tired as a Roman citizen. This great apostle was arrested, imprisoned, and threaten for the sake of the gospel. Even while on his journeys dissention arose upon those whom accompanied him but he soon reminded all of the mission. While readjusting his companions focus he then pressed forward with the original group adding other as needed. The apostle's teaching was a great call with a great responsibility that impacted the lives of many.

Newly converted Christians faced much persecution from civil and religious authorities. The first emperor to execute Christians was Herod Agrippa I (Benware 2003 p. 139) Scholars believed that Herod Agrippa I political agenda to be favorable with the Jews was the driving force behind the campaign against the Christians. The first apostle to be martyred was James. Peter would soon be thrown in prison. Some would consider this as

---

[46] ibid

a dark period in church history. (Benware 2003, 139) Even in the midst of the persecution of the church, the gospel still went out. (Acts 12:24)[47]

The Gentiles after being converted felt some persecution and conviction. (Bruce, 1988 p. 237) Though the Gentiles felt the oppression of receiving the gospel they had to their new found joy. After the Gentiles received salvation some of the Jewish followers suggest that their conversion was not authentic. The Jews suggested that all men be circumcised just as male proselytes to Judaism. (Acts 15:1)[48] Sadly, the Jews felt their heritage rendered them certain rights. Jesus being a Jew by birth was the factor used by the Jews to advocate Gentile circumcision. (Acts 15:1)[49] Though the Gentiles suffered ridicule, and ostracizing they held to their new found faith. God's desire is to take the Jew and the Gentile and make all into one new humanity being accomplished in and through Christ Jesus.

As followers of Christ, we must remember that Christ established the church and commissioned us as disciples. As He sent the disciples

---

[47] ibid
[48] King James Version. Holy Bible Grand Rapids: Zondervan 2001
[49] ibid

forth He has He sent us forth with power. The challenges faced by the disciples and Christians is their very life and their way of life. Although religious leaders challenge, provoke and oppose we must remain dedicated to the call. We can rest assured the Lord God did not leave will not leave us comfortless. The blessed hope Christians have is knowing one day Christ will return for His bride. Due to social, economic, and political views of that time receiving of the Gospel posed a threat to the recipients because of how it changed lives. One can conclude and will conclude that the political, religious and social setting of the first century has helped shaped the widespread of the gospel and its influences.

Important Issues in the Non-Pauline Churches

In the General Epistles, there exist many main themes in which the authors elaborate upon. Many controversies exist about the authorship; however the message remains the same. (Carson, D., & Moo, D. 2005) Thorough researches provide scholars the message of hope and deliverance. In each of the encounters, the author's gives enlightenments to the Christian show all a better way of life. James the brother of the Lord authored the Book of James. The theme of James provides the need for an unwavering faith. (Benware 2003 p. 240) James does not approach

doctrine concepts, however, he focus on authentication of faith.

Apparently believers were to easily taken to sinful desires with no

resistance. For faith to be appreciated in the believer's life he or she must

remain steadfast within their believers and exemplify a life of godly living.

Hebrews is the Book in which an author is not specified. (Alexander, P., &

Alexander, D. 2011) Though many have been attributed for the authoring

of Hebrews it is still unidentifiable. Hebrews introduces believers to the

saving faith of God through Jesus Christ. In addition, the believers

mention in Hebrews proves to be faithful. The purpose of Hebrews is to

show the endurance of the saints of ages past and yet remain dedicated to

our Lord.   There was a time in church history when the saints of old

suffered spiritual exhaustion. During the penning of Hebrews history, the

saints became stagnant in their faith. Spiritual exhaustion and unnurtured

faith leads to a possible of turning away from the faith.   I Peter authored

by the apostle Peter. (Benware 2003 p. 244) Peter's theme encourages

Christians to have the proper attitude and when going through persecution.

Though no child of God can avoid persecution he or she endures hardness

as a good soldier. As a Christian one must accepted and expect pain.

Although, pain is not a feeling to be desired is a too needed for proper development. It is only in our sufferings when we are made better. Adversity is a believer's mirror to his or her life. Peter impress upon the saints to preserve. II Peter authored by Apostle Peter himself. There were truths of the gospel that Peter felt the church needed reminding of: Christian development; false teachers and leaders; the character of a false teacher or leader; the understanding and assurance of Christ Return and a Christian's conduct. Jude authored Jude writing on to particulars salvation and false teachers. (Benware 2003 p. 259) This letter recorded depicts of those whom once was in the faith and departed by false teaching and or doctrine. (Beware 2003 p. 259) Jude's theme offers a contending and sound faith in the last days approaching. The Book of I, II, III John all are written by the same author, John. Each of these books is written with a different theme. I John reveal the error of an individual. John helps by providing strength if one should fall. The believer is admonished to stay in constant fellowship with God. (1 John 1:4)[50] II John theme is truth the indwelling truth. (Benware 2003 p. 264) The indwelling truth teaches a proper way of living within the truth of Jesus Christ. The Apostle John

---

[50] King James Version. Holy Bible Grand Rapids: Zondervan 2001

writings lead to an empowering truth of God's love. The truth of God will reveal and conceal. Therefore the false truths that arise from false instructors will not disturb ones inner peace. Most importantly anyone whom fails to recognize the Truth, fail to recognize the Godhead. Abiding within the truth is the desire of the author. The abiding love God will illuminate any error and lead one to a more excellent way.

The Non-Pauline Epistles are written to churches in which the Apostle Paul establishes. The Non-Pauline Epistles in comparison to the Pauline Epistles letters are different but one in the same. The Pauline epistles are: Galatians, I, II Thessalonians, I, II Corinthians, Romans, Ephesians, Colossians, Philemon, Philippians, I, II Timothy and Titus. In each of these Pauline letters, Paul provides the churches with a since of hope as he covers them. His epistles to the churches show his apostolic office. He appoints and assign trusted me to watch over the flock. He then empowers the flock and lead by visiting and encouraging. The Non-Pauline letters offers hope through a different perspective. The Non-Pauline letters are written to all for inspiration as in the Pauline epistles but to a general audience. The Pauline letters addresses a specific audience and their way of life. In addition, the non-Pauline letters offers empowerment by reflecting on the saints of ages past and how they persevered through it all. Perseverance is one of the keys to a Christian's success. Also, the general epistles present how one should live and interact as a follower of Jesus Christ.

The General Epistles (Non-Pauline Epistles) are written to provide evidence of practical conduct in one's everyday life. These books are definitely inspired by the Spirit of God. Though a few books presented the idea of known authorship it is safe to say they are inspired truths. There are truths and historical reference throughout all the epistles. Some of the author's references back to the events in the Old Testament scriptures to show the correlation between the Old Testament and the New Testament. Contrasts on false teaching and sound teachings are offered with warnings. (I Peter 1:12-21)[51] The understanding of truths is to understand the life and legacy of our Lord Christ Jesus "the anoint one". Each letter acquaints itself with the life and teachings of Christ's ministry. (Alexander, P., & Alexander, D. 2011)

---

[51] King James Version. Holy Bible Grand Rapids: Zondervan 2001

Commissioned with Resources from Christ

One must be able to know and express what resources are provided to the credential holder in ministry. The creditable minister(s) are given resources by God for their life and ministry. Jesus taught the disciples and empowered them.

- The minister is given the grace and power of Christ. The grace of God through Christ is sufficient. The power of Christ is the strength of the minister in midst of infirmities and challenging moments. When one suffers some infirmities Christ is presented with the opportunity to empower the ministers. *II Corinthians9:8, 12:9-10; I Corinthians 1:3-4[52].*

- The minister has God's presence and power with and over his life. The Holy Spirit has prepared the minister to carry out God's purpose in him. The Holy Spirit enables the minister to fulfill the ministry on earth and the power of God will rest upon the messenger. *Acts 1:8; I Corinthians 2:12.[53]*

---

[52] King James Version. Holy Bible Grand Rapids: Zondervan 2001
[53] ibid

- The minister has the presence of God and God's power. God's power and presence s sense and appreciate through His earthly vessels. The purpose of God entering man's body is to show His power by covering man's weaknesses through life no matter his obstacles. *Micah 3:8; Acts 2:25; 2 Corinthians 4:7*[54].

  1. As a minister, God rest in the heart and body of man infusing His power. The power of God is what change and transform man into a new creature. *2 Corinthians 5:17*[55]

  2. As a minister, the power of God that changes man. *Ephesians 4:24; Colossians3:10*[56]

  3. As a minister, the power of God delivers from all temptations and trials. *1 Corinthians 5:17; 2 Corinthians 2:14*[57]

  4. As a minister, the power of God that is divine nature within the minister. *2 Peter 1:4*[58]

---

[54] ibid
[55] ibid
[56] ibid
[57] ibid

5. As a minister, the power is given to the minister's life, both abundant and eternal. *John 10:10; 3:16*[59]

- The assurance given is absolute from God to the minister. It is God who causes the minister to be triumphal. The triumph is in and through Christ and Christ alone. The triumph is given to spread the glorious message of Christ all over the world. *2 Corinthians 2:14*[60]

- Spiritual Gifts are from God by God. Whatever God has given you to do he has provide through the gifts to be successful. Everything that one needs us encompassed in the spiritual gifts; spiritual office and with abilities. *Ephesians 4:11; 1 Corinthians 12:28; Romans 12:6-8*[61]

- Faith is given and needed to sustain. When all else fails the minister he must know his faith will sustain. Faith will not allow one to become discouraged nor fall into depression. It is by faith the promises of God are revealed and given. *2 Corinthians 4:13;*

---

[58] ibid
[59] King James Version. Holy Bible Grand Rapids: Zondervan 2001
[60] ibid
[61] ibid

Acts 27:25; Romans 4:20-21; Hebrews 11:6; Ephesians 6:16; 1 John 5:4-5[62]

- The love of Christ is given for ministry commission. The love of Christ sustains and constrains one in ministry. In addition, the love of Christ is the message given to spread aboard to a dying and corrupt world. *2 Corinthians 5:14* [63]

- The hope of the resurrection sustain the ministry. Therefore, a glorious day of resurrection will come. One must suffer and endure all hardness as a good soldiers. Continue to teach and preach and serve the people- because one day your day of resurrection will come. *Philippians 3:10-11*[64]

Your Daily Walk as a Minister

Though a minister is opposed with many ways of walking he must know, believe and understand God. God created the minister and saved the minister to work and point all soul unto Him.

---

[62] ibid

[63] ibid

[64] King James Version. Holy Bible Grand Rapids: Zondervan 2001

1. In daily walking as a minister the minister must desires to know Him personally and intimately.

2. Believe God. Believe and know that his love for all. Know that He is with you in al trials and temptations. Believe in your call and commission to proclaim. You must know God by revelation; He must reveal Himself to you.

3. Aim to understand God. Understand and remember that He is God alone. God is righteous, holy, loving, gracious, and just. God will judge sin and will forgive sin. God alone has saved man: therefore HE alone must be worshipped and served by man. *Isaiah 43:10; Isaiah 41:4*[65]

- Personally knowing and talking with Christ will empower the minister. As a minister, one must seek a victorious experience with Christ. His power over this world is to know along with the power of Christ resurrection. *Philippians 3:10-11; Luke 9:23; Romans 12:11*[66]

---

[65] ibid
[66] ibid

- Remembering to forget the past and press on for the prize. As a minister, you must forget the past and press forth to those things which are before you, by concentrating. Remain focus. *Philippians 3:13-14*[67]

Identity of Christ

The Christians "identity in Christ" helps distinguishes their faith group from any other. As a Christian certain characteristic and identity traits are developed. Throughout history Christians has been regarded as a people of purpose. To better understand "identity in Christ" one must see the operation of the Spirit of Christ in a believer. The operation of spiritual gifts must be exercised in the life of a believer. These spiritual gifts have been employed by Christ. Therefore, one has the ability to find his or her identity in Christ.

In Saint John Chapter 8 Jesus demonstrates a clear depiction of himself and his followers. In addition, when one believers on the Lord Jesus Christ and accepts him as Savior his or her faith must be tested and tried. The trying of a saint's faith is more precious than that of pure gold.

---

[67] King James Version. Holy Bible Grand Rapids: Zondervan 2001

Although, Jesus is a part of the Godhead he is just as much human as you and I. However, Jesus is sinless. Therefore, we the followers of Jesus Christ must adhere to all the teaching of Jesus proving our submission just as Jesus did to humanity. Disciples of Jesus Christ are established when the life of Jesus is lived through a convert individual. John's gospel focuses on the life Jesus and the infallible prove of his identity.

In a world that is vastly changing Christ often times is hard to be seen in the lives of most believers. Being children of God we must understand that Christ liberated. Then, we become empowered by the virtue of his cross and mediation, by his word and the working of the Holy Spirit. The forms of identity in Christ are revealed in the following: ones energy for the things of God; the mindset of knowing with assurance; and the evidence of boldness through Christ Jesus. Persons energetic for the things of God are demonstrating a form of identity in Christ; by regaining gainful employed in the fulfillment of ministry. A determined soul to finish the work Christ began is what he requires of believers. Though living in a world full of destructions one must keep a pure mind of perseverance. Whatsoever things is pure, lovely and good report we must think on those things. Possessing the characteristic of boldness is a sure form of identity in Christ. Wherever Christ went he was never afraid to confront issues but yet he always provided hope to all in need and desires.

Identity in Christ is a concern all followers of Jesus faces. Though there are obstacles one must at all times remember how Christ lived. Reflecting upon how our Lord lived and died provides Christians with the necessary tools to be successful while living here on earth below. Although, tools has been provided we still need to desire more of the knowledge of God and seek our Savior the more. Looking to Jesus the author and finisher of our faith ensures a successful life experience as well as a successful Christian experience. Once we adopt the idea of seeking our Savior for all directions then the true identity will be revealed in heaven and on earth.

A Will within a Will

To understand our purpose with God in our live is a serious concept of beginning. So often times we as people of God (God's Chosen) misses our bountiful blessings because we fail to find and fulfill our purpose. God has given man everything he or she needs to be successful in this present life. If one fails to develop many times his or her life becomes a life of lack. Jesus cam and live among men so that believer will have a blueprint for walking in their destiny through Him. We must change the way we walk daily. Then the Holy Spirit will and can abide. The Holy Spirit will overshadow us in order to direct us. Once we give ourselves to Jesus then and only then the Holy Spirit will be able to fulfill the destiny that God have in designed for us.

Another factor to concentrate upon is the concept of being. God has made man to be like Him. Mankind is composed of three major components soul, spirit and body. (the covering) Soul- what make us who we are; the essence of human inner. Spirit the illumination of the soul and the body to protect shell. Body the outer covering the wholes everything together that is within.

Change is inevitable. Without proper development we will live a mild nourished life, unfulfilled. Properly identifying the ideas and concepts to change will ensure a well round developed individual. Christians that fails to advance are Christian with defeated lives. Christian who fails to properly exercise their faith is being conquered from within. Identifying and recognizing opens the possibilities advance and establish.

Where there is a will there is a way. Our Lord came and lived to show us the more excellent way. The Christians life has been established to help assist and better everyday life for all through Christ giving God all the glory. Our priority is pleasing our Lord their precepts and examples.

Identification, analysis and assessment are forms of development that are crucial to a Christian life. Before, a risk and self-improvement can be, one must identify what have or what is taking place. Every day present new and different struggles. Each day a Christian operates his or her daily operation they must be aware of the potential risk or opportunities within their activities. In addition, analysis needs to be done so that one make inventory of his or her actions which will intern assist in their development. Analysis is understood to be the understanding that one has received during the reconstruction of self-improvement. Assessment are the compiling of all information that has been collected due to the identify problem.

When I consider my identity, I am so very thankful that I am securely saved in Christ. Two verses that speak to me in a mighty way as a minister of Christ are 1 Timothy 1:12 and Luke 10:20 as they speak of salvation and grace. It is the grace of God that was bestowed upon me that saved me from a certain doom, and His indwelling empowers me to do His work to the glory of God. So, it is not for the reason that I am identified as a good person that Christ has sanctified me. Yet, it is because I have answered the call and believe in Him by faith. Now, I am identified in Him and I have been sent into a lost world that they may know Jesus as well. This is all encapsulated in a verse that is never far from my heart, "I thank Christ Jesus our Lord, who has given me strength, that he considered me trustworthy, appointing me to his service" (NIV, 1 Timothy 1:12)[68]. I find this verse to be very influential as I live for the one who gave His all for me. It is a reminder that I am identified as humbly being a servant of Jesus Christ who is not to be my own bidding, but I am to be following His example and diligently be doing God's work. Jesus once told His disciples, "However, do not rejoice that the spirits submit to you,

---

[68] King James Version. Holy Bible Grand Rapids: Zondervan 2001

but rejoice that your names are written in heaven" (NIV, Luke 10:20)[69], and this applies to every Christian. As we go into the highways and byways of life, we are certainly told that we will face opposition, and I am thankful for Christ's presence in my life that grants my victory over things that are meant to destroy me. I am indeed grateful that I am saved, saved, saved forever more. I am furthermore indebted God's service as I had a debt that could not be paid, but Christ paid the sin debt in full upon the cross. Now, I rejoice to be identified with The Risen Christ who is saving me a place in heaven.

In a world where knowledge is readily available, one must be knowledgeable and learned about his or her beliefs. Proverbs4:7[70] states wisdom is the principal thing; therefore get wisdom: and with all thy getting get understand. Being able to defend one's faith is of the uttermost. Jesus Christ did what no other could have and would have done. At the place of employment, I am privileged to encounter many individuals. There are some individuals on the job whom are saved, unsaved, and even unrepented. Each day I make it my business to be available and in always

[69] ibid
[70] King James Version. Holy Bible Grand Rapids: Zondervan 2001

offering some form of good news about Jesus Christ. It is my goal and my desire that I represent Christ in all things. Many times my colleagues engage in unprofitable conservation. The majority of the persons conversing all are professing Christians. Being lead of God I am often placed in the position to remind the other saints of we are. Though we are individuals we belong to Christ; therefore, we must according to Christ's guidelines. What fellowship does light have with darkness? How can two walk together unless they agree? These are questions one should ask his or her self when working for Jesus. Then, I am met with opposition from the confessing but not possessing Christians. I inform my coworkers to remember that if salt loses its savor is of no effect. Therefore, the Christian life is to be a pattern and example to others as to who Christ is and what Christ represents. One can conclude that defending one's faith is a sign of assurance within what he or she already has obtained. Servant evangelism must become and remain a lifestyle not only to the evangelist but to the Christian.

Servant Leadership

The best leader are not only born; but shaped and molded into great men and women. A good leader can be best described as one who possesses selfless characteristics. One who put forth energy when needed brings out better and can accomplish better. In addition, leaders build people to become unified team members. Teamwork is needed in all forms or businesses and organizations. His or her attitude in team building and people reaching will ensure the success of the all corporations and organizations. An effective leader builds one on one bonds with his or her constitutes. Therefore, the leader must be willing to expand his or her skills as it relates to group work, committees, and programs by learning to function well in one to several and one to many settings. A leader must adopt a healthy management style with personnel by providing both freedom and security for all individuals. Once the leader develops the organization articulating its dream is obtainable; building trust and teamwork is also obtainable. Though varies administrative challenges arises working well with people will foster the best development for all. Although, a good leader is described by goal reaching and selfless acts he or she will obtain their set goals due to their concern is greater than themselves.

In my research and studies, I have found an ideal leader to be one who meets the ideal needs of the corporation. He or she does not necessary cares about the development of his or her people but, meeting the said goal; therefore, people building is not performed nor embraced. The ideal leader quickly reminds those associated of why they are there and the expectations expected. Working with people the ideal leader understands is a must; however, he only gives the bare minimum. This leader becomes a delegator because of his or her motivation is not into people reaching and team building.

Dealing with difficult personnel can be a strain on a business and organization. Every organization has individuals and personnel who are abrasive to the larger organization. They are not emotionally unbalanced; they are just relationally out of step with the mainstream development of business. Difficult personnel can fall into two board categories: aggressive and passive. The aggressive personnel and or individual tries to dominate the overall mission of the organization. The passive personnel and or individual places a drag on the mission and momentum of the organization. This is an area of pitfall that a leader must be made aware of. A decision must be made as to whether negative behavior can be ignored or whether it must be confronted. Also, the leader must be watchful of cliques, they can control a business atmosphere for good or ill. Dealing with pitfall is a must and if not handle correctly can be deadly to the organization future. Another area of concern is innate leadership can best be described as leadership one is born with. Those things that are innate for an individual is a part of his or her character. Therefore an individual does not have to perform an action of obtain the ability one possess. On the other hand learned leadership is leadership one must be trained and taught. Therefore, learned leadership for an individual must first begin with a desire of the work. Immediately following the desire he or she then begins practicing their desire. In most cases personality types seems to dominate over other personalities. For an example, persons whom have a level of aggression tend to make good leaders. Because they are risk takers then he or she can assume positions of leadership and make things happen. One can conclude that individuals with a good getter attitude and a level of aggression can obtain goals and become great leaders.

Reflecting upon the different examples used throughout leadership I found each of them to be fundamental. The illustration of King David show a depiction of how one can be influenced through his or her arrogance. Arrogance requires no effort but intelligence requires intellect. Individuals must be interview for the position in which he or she seeks. Most importantly persons should feel a call in their life to hold their office of choice. Along with the interview a resume must be presented to reflect their accomplishments and abilities. Arrogance is best seen when a friend or a love one place within a position but has no training or skill in the said area. In addition, a learned but called individual will offer the best wide range of knowledge to a corporation. However, a close friend or acquaintance unlearned in the business and Robert's Rules of order will sabotage a company.

In leadership there exist many functions; however, the five dysfunctional leadership styles should be avoided. The five dysfunctional leadership styles are: acknowledge your dark side; examine the past; resist the poison of expectations; practice progressive self-knowledge; and understand your identity in Christ. Acknowledging ones darks side is recognizing our sinfulness and the seeking the forgiveness and redemption that can only be found through Jesus Christ. An example of failing to acknowledge ones dark side is King David. King David tries to disassociate himself by not acknowledging his self-deception. Only after David realize the error of his ways with grievous dalliance is when he took the necessary steps in overcoming his dark side. The examining of one's past is the exploration of the periods of serious and painful reflection experienced. An example of reflecting upon such pain is the evaluating of one's current leadership and future leadership for the assignment of blame and or for self-understanding. Remembering that one cannot change his or her past but the reflecting and reminiscing upon the past overcome the influence over us. Resisting the position of expectations is laying aside the expectations impressed upon us by others. Many of us fears disappointing others; therefore we take on unnecessary weights. Though expectations allows for goal to be obtain one must be careful that the ladder of success is climbed accordingly. "Expectations can either propel people to achieve or they can produce pain and failure." (Rima and McIntosh pa. 185) For an example, some pastors have set unrealistic goals by not having proper the resources and or the means. Due to one's cumulative affects the pastor find himself declining and failing. The most severe difficulty faced today is the multiplying of intense expectations which creates a burden for all involved within the corporation.

Leaders can and will face difficulties when he or she feels to consider the group before embarking upon task. In addition, if a leader takes risk without properly considering his or people then the organization and or group will be comprised. Also, no room is left for problem solving. Problem solving is creative instead of a frustrating but a good method must be applied and not risk taking at will. Another negative draw in risk taking is it often times undermines the company and its employees. Leadership respect the God-created uniqueness of their staff and colleagues.

The Minister's Alliance to the Ministry

- The minister of Christ is to be all things a pattern to the flock, in diligence, earnestness, discretion, and punctuality. "By pureness,

knowledge, love unfeigned, the word of truth, the power of God, and the armor of righteousness on the right hand and on the left."
2 Corinthians 6:6-7[71]

- The minister of the Gospel in the church must know that he or she has peace with God, through our Lord Jesus Christ, and that he sanctified wholly by the baptism of the Holy Spirit. He must have a deep sense of the fact that souls for whom Christ died are perishing, and that he is called of God to proclaim to them the glad tidings of salvation.

- The minister must likewise have a deep sense of the necessity of believers going on unto perfection and developing the Christian graces in practical living; that their love may abound yet more in knowledge and in all judgment. He must have a strong appreciation of both salvation and Christian ethics.

- The minister must have gifts, as well as grace, for the work. He will have a thirst for knowledge, especially of the Word of God, sound judgment and good understanding. Clear views concerning the plan of redemption and salvation as revealed in scriptures.

---

[71] King James Version. Holy Bible Grand Rapids: Zondervan 2001

Saints will be edified and sinners converted through his ministry. He must be an example in prayer.

- He must be regenerated, sanctified, and baptized with the Holy Ghost before he us qualified for the charge as pastor.

- To prove that he has these qualifications, he must abstain from all appearances of evil, manifest love, mercy and judgment. "The very God of all peace sanctify you wholly and preserve him blameless until the coming of our Lord Jesus Christ."

- He must be subject to Christ who hath made us able ministers of the New Testament, not of the letter, but of the Spirit.

- The minister should give himself to prayer and to the ministry of the word, that he might know the Spirit. "For as many as are led by the Spirit of God they are the Sons of God."

To understand our purpose with God in our live is a serious concept of beginning. So often times we as people of God (God's Chosen) misses our bountiful blessings because we fail to find and fulfill our purpose. God has given man everything he or she needs to be successful in this present life. If one fails to develop many times his or her life becomes a life of lack. Jesus came and live among men so that believer will have a blueprint for walking in their destiny through Him. We must change the way we walk daily. Then the Holy Spirit will and can abide. The Holy Spirit will overshadow us in order to direct us. Once we give ourselves to Jesus then and only then the Holy Spirit will be able to fulfill the destiny that God have in designed for us.

Pastoral Epistles Teaching for the followers of Christ

The Apostle Paul the author of the Pastoral Epistles has composed an outline of instructions for leaders. Though there has been some controversy in his authorship, scholars have identified that these letters are written in the support of Pauline authorship. There are three Pastoral Epistles: I Timothy, II Timothy, and Titus. Each of the epistles concerning pastoring includes church order and discipline. The need for these Pastoral letters assisted men whom take care of the local churches and have committed themselves to the work thereof. The composing of the epistles was written while Paul was freed from imprisonment. It understood that the apostle travel extensively and yet he was composing the good news. Two major issues found in the Pastoral Epistles are conduct and false teachers.

One major area of concern the apostle taught on is false teachers and teachings. Within the Pastoral Epistles the apostle address this issue thoroughly. In I Timothy 1:3-20[72], Paul begins this letter first exhorting Timothy to address false Jewish teachers. The issue Timothy needed to address was the Jewish leaders formulating doctrine and practice off of Jewish legends and philosophies. Paul encouraged Timothy to preach the gospel stating that the Law could not save. These Jewish leaders were preaching the Old Testament covenant and did not recognize the new dispensation of grace. The Apostle Paul referenced to himself as to how he attempted to be a law keeper and unknowingly could not do so. Finally, overseer Paul encouraged Timothy to preach sound doctrine both in I Timothy and II Timothy. In Titus 1:10-16[73], Paul empowers Titus to guard the flock. The church is to be protected by the pastor. He then encourages Titus to not allow false teaching to arise among the brethren. Titus instructions were to

---

[72] King James Version. Holy Bible Grand Rapids: Zondervan 2001
[73] King James Version. Holy Bible Grand Rapids: Zondervan 2001

preach faith in God through Christ Jesus. In preaching faith in God, Titus would be able to ward off any false teachings and teachers. He established and delegated administration and authority throughout the church. The apostle emphasizes leadership and their need to preach the truth of God.

Godly conduct is another area of concern in which the apostle taught. There must be found godly living in the church among the leadership. (Titus 2:1, 15)[74] Under-shepherds are to teach with authority the mysteries of God while correctly living. The seasoned men of the church are to be disciplined and sound. The younger adult men must demonstrate self-control and a willingness to be taught. The younger brethren are to be the leaders in collective prayers. (I Timothy 2:8)[75] After leading prayer, the brethren should pray for the people's salvation and covering, therefore the gospel message will spread aboard. The aged women of the church are to be modest and found giving instructions to younger women. Women of God are to be found in good modest apparel. The beauty of a woman is the apple of her

---

[74] ibid
[75] ibid

husband's eye, but she must be presentable. Too much apparel without modesty is a distraction in the worship of God. The women should not be found in gossip. (Titus 2:2-10)[76] The apostle informed the women of God of their position in the public and in the church. (I Timothy 2:11-15)[77] The godly woman should be apt to learn and not be the authoritative figure with doctrine. (Benware 2003 p. 227) The New Testament teaching is required to be taught with authority. Therefore she cannot be a teacher of doctrine. The Apostle Paul made specific notation that a woman's sphere is the home and this is our greatest contentment. The instructing of the leaders life in the church also include the offices of deacons and elders. These are two offices the apostle expounded upon. Deacons and elders must be men of a good report and full of integrity in order to be assess the local church administration. The Elders must teach by precepts and examples. These are men whom are versed in scripture and learned leaders. Although no man can obtain perfection, the men of God must remain humble.

---

[76] ibid
[77] King James Version. Holy Bible Grand Rapids: Zondervan 2001

The local churches are governed similarly like to the churches of ages past. However, some organizations and administrations handle issues differently. For instance, the Congregationalist churches allow the local board of deacons or elected officials to govern the administration of the church. With the Congregationalist system the Pastor is limited mostly to preaching the gospel. In many Pentecostal organizations an Episcopal system of government is used. The Board of Bishops is the ecclesiastical governing agent of their churches. In each of these bodies of believers their conduct emulates the early Christian church. Both them have a governing oversee which includes a collective group. The collective groups are representation of the apostle's covering to the original churches. Due to the modernization of today's churches the conduct and discipline are handled on an as needed basis.

The Pastoral Epistles serves as a model for today and future leaders of the church. The hidden mysteries of God are in the heart of the chosen leader. Since the early existences of the church men have followed this set pattern of instructions. The Apostle Paul gave instructions to assist a leader in his conduct and in his teachings. These epistles are given to exhort all to guard the truth of God but teach the doctrine of God. A man and woman of God must be grounded in order for the ministry to reach all. The importance of proper administration, godly living, and proper teaching will allow the local ministry be most effective in today's church. The Pastoral Epistles lays the foundation for a success ministry.

The early Christians and the church had practical issues that Apostle Paul addressed. In the Pauline Epistles, Paul addressed the church at Corinth and the issues this young reformation faced. (Carson & Moo 2005) The founding of the church of Corinth took place during his second missionary journey. The Apostle Paul's dedication to the believers at Corinthian is a good depiction of an overseer's care and concern. The purposes for Corinthian epistle encompass sanctification and reconciliation. Sanctification is being set a part. Reconciliation is to remove enmity between individuals or parties. Man must be reconciled back to God through sanctification. The apostle's writing of I Corinthians is, first to prove instructions on how to handle severe problems in the church and second, to provide doctrinal clarity for new converts. The recordings of II Corinthians were written to reestablish authority and to establish order for preservation of the church.

Corinth was a city known for its corruption and political influence. Living in Corinth offered a life of luxury. To better understand this wealthy city is to understand Roman rule which in encompasses sexual immortality. There is no doubt while the church at Corinth experienced problems with immorality. In addition, he references Jesus Christ as being the head of the church. Then, Paul encourages all to be in fellowship. (I Cor. 1:9)[78] As the apostle continues to write he empowers and establishes sound doctrine for believers to adhere too. Paul was well aware that the Corinthian believers were spiritual gifted and talented. He reminds them while they are awaiting the Lord's return believers must remain proactive until Jesus comes.

The Corinthian Church still faced issues during the writings of II Corinthians. (Benware 2003 p.185) The Apostle Paul appointed Titus

---

[78] King James Version. Holy Bible Grand Rapids: Zondervan 2001

to go assist at Corinth. (II Corinthians 2: 12-13)[79] Paul reaffirmed the

Corinthian church that the ultimate authority in the church is Jesus

Christ the Lord. The troubles arising in the church had to be

controlled. The Corinthian saints were reminded of giving to the poor

and needy in Judea and repentance. A genuine passion for the gospel

ministry is what the apostle preached. As Paul seeks to provide in-

depth understanding to the church he addresses the following areas:

teachings about true ministry, exhortations, instructions about giving,

and the apostolic ministry. The Church at Corinth is addressed by the

Apostle Paul to be saved. (I Cor. 1:2-4)[80]

The doctrine taught by the apostle targeted specific areas of

concern as they relate to what Jesus taught. Paul pinpointed the

manner an individual responds to the Word of God. If a believer fails

to live upright he or she will become an undeveloped Christian

spiritually. A believer must allow the Word of God to become alive in

him. (I Cor. 2:14-3:4)[81] Knowledge appropriation gives an individual

---

[79] ibid
[80] ibid
[81] ibid

119

spiritual development where they can grow productively. Jesus taught that "Man cannot live by bread alone but by every word that proceed out of the mouth of God." (Matt. 4:4)[82] The apostle Paul reminded believers the knowledge of God is the cross of Christ. It is the transformation of power that salvation provided through the workings of Christ. (II Cor. 3:4-18)[83] Therefore an individual can only see his need for Christ when he views the cross of Calvary. This is the message Christ preached and taught as he walked among men. Hebrews 9:22[84].....Without the shedding of blood there is no remission of sin.

Christian theology can be gathered from Paul's teachings. First, he offered the believer in instructions on morals and discipline. (I Cor. 5:1-3)[85] Second, he addresses immorality in the church and how it should not be. (I Cor. 6:12-20)[86]. His next area of concern is the

---

[82] King James Version. Holy Bible Grand Rapids: Zondervan 2001
[83] ibid
[84] ibid
[85] ibid
[86] ibid

problems of those in ministry; matters of marriage (I Cor.7:1-40)[87]; matters of doubtful things (I Cor.8:1-11:1)[88]; matters of worship and ministry (I Cor. 11-2-14:40)[89] and the matter of resurrection (I Cor. 15:1-58)[90] finally, the personal suffering required of a child of God. The Christian's perspective desire is to be bondslave to Christ. The Christian theology as the apostle taught informs the believers as to his sacrifices of pleasure and gain. In addition, the apostle final thought was repent and turn away from sin. As believers we must realize our need for God and our insufficiencies; therefore the power of God can rest upon us.

The writing of this Corinthian letter was written during a turmoil and conflict with some individuals within the Corinthian church. However, the Apostle Paul expresses deep passion within this epistle to encourage wholeness. Paul's heartfelt emotions are moved due to all the conflict the church experiences. At the same time, joy is felt by the apostle his desire was not for himself but for God's glory in him

---

[87] ibid
[88] ibid
[89] ibid
[90] ibid

through Jesus Christ. It is interesting to note that the Apostle Paul wrote this to the Romans from Corinth. His writings were not for the Corinthians, the Jews and the Greeks along but for all follower of Christ the Lord. Because of the depravity of man the apostle saw the need to write and build the ministry.

The apostolic authority in which the Apostle Paul exercised was shepherd hood. This act of authority is depicted as one whom covers and sacrifices himself for his own. Paul's interaction with the converts can is a present day illustration of a pastor covering the members of his ministry. The apostle is a representative of the Lord Jesus. The apostle proved the gospel to be the infallible proof of Christ. However, he receives no credit and seeks no recognition. It is the genuine love the apostle demonstrates that allows all to see the love of God disbursed abroad. The churches in Corinth was not established and left unattended but overseen by its founder.

Chapter Five Summary and Conclusions

Mentoring Program of Ministerial &Ministry Ethics

I.   *Mentoring Program Ministry Guidelines:*

An effective church Administrator must learn to build one on one

relationships with all members within the local congregations. Also,

leaders must be willing to explore concepts in group work, ministry

committees, and program councils. Working with church people and

or Christians involves a variety of administrative challenges.

Therefore, mentor serves as a sponsor, guide, model and cheerleader.

The novice receives encouragement, nourishment, guidance and

proven way of working.

Leadership Development

•   All mentors chosen and or selected for mentoring ministry must

understand the nature of their call. One must examine himself and make sure that he or she continues in the faith of Christ. (2 Corinthians 13:5)[91]

Understanding Congregations as Service Organizations. (Romans 12:1-2)[92]

    a. Church and other Christian institutions fit into the not-for-profit category. They exist to render service. The mission of many churches is often unattainable in the short run. Most churches pays their leaders poorly and sometimes recruit their volunteers on an "anybody we can get to do the job" basis.

1. Leading through Committees (I Corinthians 12:13-17)[93]

    b. Keep these things in mind as you work with church committees:

        i.   Committees exist for church and ministry (ethics), not vice versa.

        ii.   Committees have no life independent of the people.

---

[91] King James Version. Holy Bible Grand Rapids: Zondervan 2001
[92] ibid
[93] ibid

      iii.   Committees are to help the larger body of believers through the ministry.

      iv.   Congregations owe its committees a job description, and a forum for reporting their work.

2. Paying Volunteers

    a. Volunteers do not receive wages, fringe benefits or bonus. But they do receive emotional and spiritual rewards. Volunteers are paid –in service, recognition, growth, challenge, results, love and teamwork.

3. Building a Unified Team for Leadership (Ephesians 4:12)[94]

    a. Teamwork is needed in the congregation anytime two or more people must work together and depend on each other.

    b. One key attitude in team building and kingdom reaching is making ministry results the captain of the team. Goals become the focus of team building with individual goals and other concerns being secondary.

    c. Several ingredients are basic to developing an effective team. They are:

---

[94] King James Version. Holy Bible Grand Rapids: Zondervan 2001

     i.   Clearly defined expectations.

     ii.   Settings where people feel free to risk their ideas and concerns.

     iii.   Cooperation rather than competition.

     iv.   Commitment to congregational goals.

4. Solving Problems as a Leader (James 1:5)[95]

   a. Every leader/ minister faces problems. Problems solving can become creative instead of a frustration experience if a good method is used.

   b. Begin with a concise and precise statement of the problem.

   c. Brainstorm possible solutions by "goals wishing."

5. Managing Leadership Meetings (I Corinthians 11:1-5)[96]

   a. Ministers and Mentors alike must guide meetings well or risk losing volunteers. Avoid extra unnecessary meetings.

   b. Meetings are necessary when:

     i.   Staff and or members concerns needs to be discussed

---

[95] King James Version. Holy Bible Grand Rapids: Zondervan 2001
[96] ibid

ii.   Consensus building is needed.

iii.   Verbal reports to be cultivated.

iv.   Many members need training at the same time.

c. Effective meeting need a plan or model to be used in guiding the progress of the meeting.

    i.   Evaluate the group's progress towards it mission.

    ii.   Create a range of options and resources for dealing with challenges.

    iii.   Decide which alternative to recommend for the ministry consideration.

    iv.   Implement the mentors ministry decisions and programs.

6. Chairing Decision-making Meetings (Proverbs 3:1-8)[97]

a. Formal decision-making meetings can be intimidating. Some straightforward principles can be helpful.

    i.   Limit discussion to one subject at a time.

    ii.   Provide every member an equal right to speak.

    iii.   Offer motions and vote.

---

[97] ibid

  iv. Allow for full and free discussion.

  v. Protect the rights of the majority and minority.

  vi. Set the climate for teamwork, cooperation and consideration.

 b. The duties of the Chairperson usually include:

  i. Keeping the meeting moving according to agenda.

  ii. Knowing the bylaws and rules

  iii. Acting fairly and striving to preserve harmony.

7. Relating to Church Staffers (Romans 12:5-8)[98]

 a. Leaders should respect the God created uniqueness of their staff and colleagues.

 b. They should help them grow, meet their needs, and reach personal and congregations goals.

 c. They must maintain a corporate perspective and view the congregation's needs in its broadest scope.

 d. Every staff person should know the descriptions of the job responsibilities so that other staff and congregation alike will know the expectations.

98

e.   Leaders must adopt a healthy management style with

staffers by providing both freedom and security for

workers.

•   All mentors must possess a level of dedication. Though one may

enjoy his or her call of duty dedication is required to receive maximum

results. One must always seek first the kingdom of God and His

righteousness. (Matthews 6:33)[99]

•   All mentors counselor are ask to adhere to the loyalty policy. All

mentees will need to know they matter in order to gain and to be

rehabilitated. One must live a crucified life in Christ and of self-denial

and sacrifice. (Luke. 9:23)[100]

•   All mentors commitment is a must when one works in the ministry

of helps. One must arm his or her self with the whole armour of God

and be strong in Christ. (Ephesians 6:10-18)[101]

---

[99] King James Version. Holy Bible Grand Rapids: Zondervan 2001
[100] ibid
[101] ibid

- All mentors must at all times provide compassion and consideration. One must be sure that he or she is a new creation in Christ Jesus.(Ephesians 4:22-24)[102]

- All mentors must guide the meetings well or risk losing volunteers. Avoid extra and unnecessary meetings. (1 Corinthians 11: 1-5)[103]

II. Mentoring Program Ministry Plan:

Formal decision-making meetings can be intimidating. Some straightforward principles can be helpful. It is designed for relating to each other effectively in order to do the work of the Lord. In addition, help the church understand its mission and its priorities through developing men and women to become greater.

- Prayer--having a prayer life ensure for a success in marriage and ministry. One must pray always moment by moment striving to gain an unbroken consciousness of the Lord. (Colossians 4:2-4)[104]

1.   Remain steadfast in prayer

---

[102] ibid
[103] ibid
[104] King James Version. Holy Bible Grand Rapids: Zondervan 2001

2. Develop an attitude of prayer

3. Walk in the spirit of prayer

•Studying the Word (Bible)--God will direct children by speaking from His word; therefore His children must know His Word. (2 Timothy 3:16)[105]

      1. Develop obsession for the Word of God

      2. Reprove to stir a person to prove himself through the Word.

      3. Exhort through the Word of God by beseeching encouraging and comforting,

- Understanding your Purpose - -Every life God has created he said it was good and very good. (1 Tim. 1:16; 1 Tim. 4:12)[106]

      1. To be an example of the glorious truth that God saves and keeps.

      2. Encourage all become discipline disciples.

      3. To teach the willing believer all one know.

- *Involvement in Ministry* –Being actively involved in ministry allows a Christian to work in his or her calling which helps one fulfill their purpose. (Col. 1:28)[107]

---

[105] ibid

[106] ibid

1.   Encourage all become discipline disciples.

2.   All men are to be seen reachable and presented
        perfect before the Lord.

3.   Be a witness for the Lord Jesus Christ.

III.   *Application of Spiritual Formation:*

To provide counseling and mentoring to all Christian and non-Christian individuals. We as a body of believers holds to the fundamental truths of the word of God. It is our belief that scriptural teaching will impact the growth, development and sense of worth to all whom seeks to become better.   To develop men to become better husbands and wives to become better women. With the proper direction and instructions all persons can be rehabilitated and empowered. The Word of God provides us with how to live and walk with Christ daily. We are to be consistent, obedient, and faithful which is what God expects. When we do what God has instructed, we then produces the most fulfilling and fruitful life and ministry.

---

[107] ibid

Spiritual formation had broadened the scope for me in the areas of church administration. In ordered for a ministry to be productive and influential the spiritual formation principles must be and should be applied within the local church's ministry. Though we are serving a risen Lord is a spirit also. They that worship him must worship Him in Spirit and in truth. Jesus is the way the truth and the light. Another area of reflection one benefited from is mentoring. To properly mentor one must first be an example of love and compassion. Love and compassion is two important qualities our Lord offers to us as Christians. Therefore, mentoring can only be beneficial when the mentor esteem the mentee higher than his or her selves.

Spiritual growth to me is a period in which a believer advances to a higher level in spirituality. As one soul's prosperous so does everything about the individual. Also, spiritual growth is spiritual maturity in God. If one fails to grow in God, the he or she fails to achieve and receive their maximum potential. It is my belief that saints has been given the best gift that any can obtain the Gift of God. Jesus

Christ was sent to redeem and restore man back to God. Through much prayer and faith God will enable mankind to do that which he has called him to do. Sure there will be times of difficulties ahead but Jesus promised to never to leave us alone. We have the Holy Spirit here with us to help aid us in our good and bad times. Spiritual growth encompasses development in ones walk with God through faith, and commitment to all that God has promised through Jesus Christ.

The work of the Holy Spirit in the life of a believer is crucial to spiritual formation. Apart from the work of the Holy Spirit there is no true spiritual formation. Paul wrote, "What we have received is ... the Spirit who is from God, so that we may understand what God has freely given us. This is what we speak ... in words taught by the Spirit, explaining spiritual realities with Spirit-taught words. The person without the Spirit does not accept the things that come from the Spirit of God but considers them foolishness, and cannot understand them because they are discerned only through the Spirit" (1 Corinthians 2:12-14)[108].

The biggest problem with seeing spiritual formation in the western church are the false ideas that either the natural realm is more real than the spirit realm or that there is no spirit realm. This is a direct result of the powerlessness of the church and the reliance on technology and medicine. However God's plan for our lives is eternal, and it has been established in the spirit realm from before the foundation of the world. (Revelation 13:8)[109] The process of the Holy Spirit working in the believer to bring about the plan of God and image of Jesus is a part of God's kingdom come to the earth and His will done on earth as they both already exist in the spirit realm. This is why Solomon wrote, "That which is has been already and that which will be has already been, for God seeks what has passed by" (Ecclesiastes 3:15)[110]. It has already passed by in the spirit realm, and God is looking for people

---

[108] King James Version. Holy Bible Grand Rapids: Zondervan 2001
[109] ibid
[110] King James Version. Holy Bible Grand Rapids: Zondervan 2001

who will allow His Spirit to bring those things into the natural realm through their lives.

I have sought in my life to submit fully to the Holy Spirit and allow Him to live through me. I always look to the Spirit to hear what heaven is saying before I make a decision. Paul wrote that faith comes by hearing the rhema from God, and the Holy Spirit makes that is possible (Romans 10:17, John 14:26)[111]. He is able to lead me to make a decision that may even seem counter intuitive because he knows what is to come (John 16:13)[112]. It's also by the Spirit that I can know the Father and the Son and grow in that relationship (Ephesians 1:17)[113].

In the sports world there is a saying that goes, "no pain no gain". Now in the realm of spiritual discipline, the sentiment is somewhat of the same. A Christian must be willing to go through the riggers of faithful training to gain the discipline necessary to live a spiritual life. Jesus said the Christian life of discipline is an ongoing process, "And

---

[111] ibid
[112] ibid
[113] ibid

he said to them all, If any man will come after me, let him deny himself, and take up his cross daily, and follow me." (Luke 9:23,KJV)[114]. He made it clear that we are to abstain from evil on a daily basis, and take up the work that has been given to him/her according to the grace of God. In this way we can be imitators of Christ and so if we look at how he lived His life, we will see how to live a spiritually disciplined life. He seperated himself from sin and communicated with the Father every step of the way and this made His the most disciplined man of all times. Now was He God or man? Yes!! He was both. He was tempted as a man but stayed holy because He was God in the flesh. He prayed. He studied. He resisted. He encourages us to do the same in His name. There are a few steps one could take to implement spiritual disciplines in their life. First, one must identify what areas of their life warrant change. This will allow the believer to review the spiritual disciplines to identify deficiencies. Once the areas have been identified, they should see which disciplines will help them to grow in specific areas. If needed, the believer should consult their pastor or other believers. Finally, they should begin

---

[114] ibid

practicing those disciplines. The believer has to understand that change will not happen overnight; with prayer, patience, and time, the process will become easier. Believers must be mindful of Paul's words when practicing spiritual disciplines, "I press toward the mark for the prize of the high calling of God in Christ Jesus" (Philippians 3:14, KJV)[115].

In today's world where diversity is present and prevalent to know God and possess the knowledge of God is necessary. Having the knowledge of God and applying it to one's life will leave to a life of enrichment. Theologians can agree that practicing believers whom operate in the knowledge and ideas of the triune God have a more productive life. In addition, leading men and women of God are yet proving to the world that serving the triune God (the only wise God) has its benefits and endless possibilities. "Now unto him that is able to keep you from falling, and to present you faultless before the presence of his glory with exceeding joy, to the only wise God our Savior, be

---

[115] King James Version. Holy Bible Grand Rapids: Zondervan 2001

glory and majesty, dominion and power, both now and ever. Amen (KJV, Jude 1: 24, 25)[116]

Theologians throughout the ages have acclaimed and tested that God is indeed exist and is God. Many questions and concern has arisen concerning God and what He is like. The great theologians of our time and ages past have tackled the idea. Every theologian's research and study the methodology of God gave insight to consider. It is safe to receive every theologian's ideology when it leads one to know God more intimately. Each of these scholars of scripture arrives at the same ideas. Though theologian's opens individual's hearts and mind to the reality of a true and living God there process of reaching and obtaining one must be sure it is bible based. Due to the fact that each scholar have a different channel of reaching does mean he or she has no bases. Throughout the centuries mankind has tried his or her best to depict who they believe God to be. "Ask and it shall be given you; seek, and ye shall find; knock, and it shall be opened to you."

---

[116] King James Version. Holy Bible Grand Rapids: Zondervan 2001

(NKJV, Matthew 7:7)[117] Theologians have helped shape the thinking of Bible believing saints; therefore a deeper hunger and thirst is introduced to an individual to encourage them the more Present day theologians of today's society such as R.C. Sproul, Pleasing God; Ravi Zacharias; Can Man Live Without God? Milliard J. Erickson, Does It Matter If God Exists?   The selected theologians mention above elaborates upon shares interesting concepts and precepts that all Bible believers should consider. These chosen theologians introduce ideas of the Trinity but yet different viewpoints from one another. One thing for sure is that each of them agrees that God does exist and He is the Almighty Creator. Zacharias offer up the idea that philosophically man cannot live or mere exit without a God. Erickson asks the question does it even matter if God exist. Then, theologian Sproul states "we don't have a natural inclination to honor a holy God." Within each argument and subject matter presented one is challenged to see the comparing and contrasting of the Trinity but realizes that no any one person truly have the answer.

---

[117] ibid

Though there are several controversies within the theological world, Bible believers are encouraged to seek God and then allow the witness within them (the Holy Spirit) to lead and guide one into truth. Present day theologians and theologians of ages past all have accomplished their mission when Christians seek to know more about Christ. There is an internal yearning that all God can bring peace. The Godhead is revealed in and through nature the more one yearns the more he or she will be filled. "Blessed are those who hunger and thirst for righteousness, for they will be filled." (NIV, Matthew 5: 6)[118] In an every changing world where men and women, boys and girls, are constantly evaluate who they are and their purposes can find answers, peace, and contentment in the triune God. When one never ceases to know God, then he or she will begin to know Him more and more.

Establishing and Building Relationships

The older one becomes the more they realize and cherish the importance of life and how short it really is. So, many individuals are consumed with living the best possible life that they can live to reach

---

[118] King James Version. Holy Bible Grand Rapids: Zondervan 2001

ultimate happiness and achievement. However, we cannot live on this earth alone. We must live our lives and share this earth with other human beings. So, we must endeavor to learn how to live the most positive and productive lives while incorporating other human beings along this journey called life. Moreover, the world is made up of various kinds of friendships and relationships. These friendships and relationships are formed in varied environments within societies and among various kinds of people. Because we are all individuals, we are all very different. Therefore, we do not all think alike or have similar goals, interests, or characteristics. These relationships and friendships that we build have different characteristics, needs, expectations and communication involved. How each person nurtures and values these friendships and relationships can be extremely diverse. Our individual personalities also affect the way that we interact, solve problems, and respond to the many relationships and friendships that we form. However, we are most comfortable around individuals that share similar perspectives and interests as we do. Our mindsets, perceptions, and ideas can greatly hinder our expectations of any relationship or friendship. These various mindsets, perceptions, and ideas are formed and highly motivated by our cultures and societal environments and influences.

The five factors of personal attraction can also greatly affect any friendship or intimate relationship. The proximity factor deals with the geographical location of individuals. When people see each other in a variety of environments such as work, and living, they are more likely to become attracted to one another. So, the geographical locations allow individuals to interact on a more frequent basis and strong friendships and bonds can more easily form. We therefore become more familiar and comfortable with these individuals. Research shows that people become attracted to those who are similar to them, and are more satisfied in relationships with similar others. (Specher, 1981) These similarities seem to exist when individuals have leisure interests and sociocultural backgrounds factors. Fondness can be established between individuals when they share familiar environments and interests. Similarity factors exist when people like who like them. These individuals have similar interests such as age, social class, education, intelligence, and religion. Individuals feel comfortable around people that have similar values and beliefs as them. Moreover, these similarities help produce positive self-esteem, and they enjoy each other's company and companionship. Because partners spend so much time together, their similarities may increase over time. Therefore, partners are highly likely to engage in similar activities and communication styles.

The social exchange theory and the equity theory establish the many reasons why individuals start, maintain, or even end relationships. Before an individual decides to initiate a relationship, they consider what they will gain or lose by establishing the relationship. They will weigh the pros and the cons and also evaluate the relationship based on past relationships to measure expected outcomes. Individuals consider the rewards that they stand to gain by initiating a relationship. In addition, people tend to stay in relationships that they have invested the most time, energy and finances to. (Lawler and Thye, 1999) They do not want to perceive their relationship as a waste of time, money, or energies. So, if one is gaining from the relationship, they are certainly willing, remaining, and maintaining the relationship. These perspectives concerning what is worth investing in when it comes to a relationship must be established at the very beginning. Each partner has various expectations and perspectives that they bring into a relationship. So, it is important that each person is clear about these perspectives and expectations before they decide to go into a committed relationship. If these factors are not closely and seriously considered, relationships can end very abruptly and negatively.

Individuals like to feel that they are equal partners within a relationship. The equity theory states that people will remain in relationships that they achieve a certain level of satisfaction in. This satisfaction is based on costs and benefits. These benefits can be described as what the individual actually gains and costs are defined as how money, time, and energy are invested within the relationship. Individuals must feel an equilibrium concerning costs and rewards. Many relationships have ended over finances and one individual feeling as though they share the bulk of responsibility within the relationship. This is also when varying perceptions play a part. Many individuals feel differently about gender roles. Some people believe that women should be required to do the majority of domestic responsibilities within the home. If these roles and perspectives are not established at the onset of a relationship, problems may arise. Egalitarianism within a romantic relationship has been linked with greater relationship satisfaction for both men and women. (Glenwright, and Fowler, 1981) This theory produces a sense of fairness and proportion of duties for each individual within the relationship.

The penetration theory deals with partner's self-disclosure. Individuals share aspects about themselves to each other. This allows individuals to become and share intimate details about each other's lives. This process allows couple to become interdependent and involve each other in areas of their life. However, men and women may define intimacy differently. Women view intimacy as more face to face interactions while men view intimacy as any form of working or playing together. Intimacy can also be achieved by communicating from the heart about feelings and past experiences, facing problems as a team and develop spiritual/religious practices. Young couples that regularly engaged in prayer found that they were happier, satisfied, and respected their committed relationships. (Glenwright and Fowler, 1981) Prayer was viewed by these couples as a contribution to their love for each other.

Attachment styles play a huge factor in relationship building/establishment. These attachment patterns are established in early childhood. When a person has a secure attachment pattern, they are secure, confident, and can very easily with others. (Firestone, 2013) These individuals feel secure and connected with each other and free within their relationships. They have a high level of inner peace and optimism. Anxious preoccupied attachment individuals tend to be desperate and line in fantasy situations. They seek safety and emotional completeness within their partner. Furthermore, they do not feel a sense of real love and trust within their relationships. So, they very often push people away by their insecure actions. This type of behavior would greatly hinder the level of intimacy within a relationship as well trust and security. Individuals would be greatly motivated to evaluate the pros and the cons for remaining in such a stressful and insecure relationship.

Because we live in such a diverse society, we are all very different characteristics, beliefs, and perspectives. All of these aspects are vital in forming and maintaining friendships as well as relationships. The five factors of personal attraction contribute many factors that determine if and how long these relationships and friendships will exist. No matter what type of relationship or friendship that one is in, much work, effort, time, and attention is required. However, similar goals and the understanding of personal perspectives are also crucial in the maintenance of secure relationships as well as friendships.

Throughout the history of humans sin has been a battle and an ongoing struggle. Some theologians believe sin to be a disease that is curable through Jesus Christ. Humans have inherited and imputed sin. Placher states "to be born is to be a sinner." (Placher, 2003 p. 139) The very nature of mankind is to satisfy itself. "Sin is the willfulness to decide to place ones will above God's will. The nature to sin cannot be addressed only as an expression but a choice. We must understand and realize that sin is in direct enmity with God. To understand the inheritance of sin, one must first consider the concept of sin. "For as in Adam all die, so in Christ all will be mad alive." (1 Corinthians 15:22)[119] Man has been provided a way to inherit righteousness through Christ Jesus. Sin is an incapability that man faces and cannot fix. In addition, sin is a situation where man is

---

[119] King James Version. Holy Bible Grand Rapids: Zondervan 2001

efforts alone are useless. "For just as through the disobedience of the one man the many were made sinners, so also through the obedience of the one man the many will be made righteous. (Romans 5:19)[120] Wrongdoings are anything that goes against the very nature of God's holiness. Due to our fore parents, Adam and Eve's disobedience and selfishness affect the whole race of mankind. It is understood that the penalty of sin is death spiritual and natural. Though we were born sinners we do not have to remain sinners. We must realize our most holy God has made provisions for man to be redeemed. Many converted believers whom once sinners wrote songs of praise to God which is known as hymns and anthems. These hymns consist of holy anthems of reverence to His holiness Jehovah God. Then, there are those hymnologists whom wrote and write about how God delivers and sets free from sin.

There exist several hymns written by great men and women who can attest to God's saving power from the clutches of sin. Hymns can be dated back to the early years of the New Testament Church. The word hymns are derived from the Greek word "hymnos." Hymnos means song

---

[120] King James Version. Holy Bible Grand Rapids: Zondervan 2001

149

of praise and adoration. The scriptures noted that Jesus and the disciples'

song hymns. (Matthew 26:30)[121] There is not much detailed information

on hymns accept that from the first few centuries of the church. Martin

Luther is hymnologist who composed hymns from scripture. Martin

Luther is accredited as to writing and composing hymns like: O for a

Thousand Tongues to Sing; Hark the Herald Angel Sing; Christ the Lord

is risen today are all Luther's great masterpieces. In addition to those

hymns mention, there are thousands upon thousands great hymns. Hymns

such as: Nothing but the Blood of Jesus; At the Cross; At Calvary; Blest

be the ties that Binds; Love Lift me; Jesus paid it All; Great is Thy

Faithfulness; O For a Thousands Songs to Sing; Jesus Lover of my Soul;

He Lifted Me has been known to lift heavy burdens. There is a story a

message in every hymn that has been and is written. "What can wash away

my sin? Nothing but the blood of Jesus." This hymn gives special

reference to the power of the blood of Jesus and how it works.

......without the shedding of blood there is no forgiveness of sins.

(Hebrews 9:22)[122] "At the cross, at the cross where I first saw the light

---

[121] ibid

[122] King James Version. Holy Bible Grand Rapids: Zondervan 2001

and the burdens of my heart rolled away. It was there by faith I received

my sight, and now I am happy all the day!" Here the hymnologist focuses

on the Jesus redemptive power of the cross. …the cross is foolishness' to

those who are perishing, but to us who are being saved it the power of

God. (1 Corinthians 1: 18)[123] "Mercy there was great and race was free,

pardon there was multiplied to me, there my burden soul found liberty At

Calvary." Jesus, our Lord here in this song is being depicted as bearing

the agony and ridicule sin leaves on sinners. By Jesus going on up to

Calvary is bearing every burden that man could ever feel. "Blest be the

ties that binds our hearts in Christian love; the fellowship of kindred minds

is like to that above." When man walk in the newness in which Christ has

made him free then he can and will walk in blest tie of perfect harmony.

"Jesus paid it all, all to him I owe. Sin had left a crimson stain He washed

it white as snow." Jesus paid the debt that no human could pay. Jesus the

Son of God redeems man back to God in which He (Jesus) became the

ransom. "Loved lifted me, love lifted me when nothing else could help

love lifted me."

---

[123] ibid

As one compare and contrast the theology of the hymnbook to the theology of Genesis 1-11[124] the mighty hand of God can be seen and appreciated. God has spoken to man, and the Bible is His Word given to us to make wise unto salvation. God is Lord and King over his world; He rules all things for His own glory, displaying His perfections in all He does in order that men and angels may worship and adore Him throughout Genesis 1. God is Savior, active in sovereign love through the Jesus Christ to rescue believers from the guilt and power of sin to adopt us as His children. The Triune God is seen throughout Genesis, the beginning. The works of salvation is seen in and through Genesis; in addition, one can see in which all three of the Godhead together; the father offers redemption, Jesus the Son security and the Holy Spirit the applier. Therefore, one can see the comparison and contrasting of theology of the hymns as they relate to sin.

When one consider the hymns sacredness flash before the soul's eyes. To consider the awesomeness of God and His saving grace extended through Jesus ones very soul cries "Holy, holy, holy Lord God Almighty."

---

[124] ibid

Upon the fall of man sin has passed through to all generations and the Propitiator Jesus has come and made all things accessible. The penalty for sin is a high debt that only one could pay. When the blood of heifers, goats and bulls failed God sent His Son in the likeness of sinful flesh and through flesh He condemned sin. Only the Blood of Jesus could paid the most high debt man owed. Therefore, the sacredness of the hymns allows the mind of the saved sinner to reflect back on how loving and compassionate God is. Men and women, boys and girls must realize we owe God our very lives. "For whosesoever will save his life shall lose it: and whosoever will lose his life for my sake shall find it." (Matthew 16:25)[125]

---

[125] King James Version. Holy Bible Grand Rapids: Zondervan 2001

Outline of Revelation

II.   The Person of Christ (Revelation 1:9-20)[126]

III.   The Seven Churches of Asia Minor (Revelation 2:1-3:22)[127]

- o   Church of Ephesus (Revelation 2:1-7)[128]

- o   Church of Smyrna (Revelation 2:8-11)[129]

- o   Church of Pergamum (Revelation 2:12-17)[130]

- o   Church of Thyatira (Revelation 2:18-19)[131]

- o   Church of Sardis (Revelation 3:1-6)[132]

- o   Church of Philadelphia (Revelation 3:7-13)[133]

- o   Church of Laodicea (Revelation 3:14-22)[134]

---

[126] King James Version. Holy Bible Grand Rapids: Zondervan 2001
[127] ibid
[128] ibid
[129] ibid
[130] ibid
[131] ibid
[132] ibid
[133] ibid
[134] ibid

IV.   The Things to Come

   o   Heavenly Jerusalem (Revelation 4:1-5:14)[135]

   o   Seven Seals (Revelation 6:1-8:1)[136]

   o   Seven Trumpets (Revelation 8: 2-11:19)[137]

   o   Important Persons (Revelation 12:1-14:20)[138]

   o   Seven Bowls (Revelation 15:1-16:21)[139]

   o   Two Babylons (Revelation 17:1-18:24)[140]

   o   Final Visions (Revelation 19:1-22:5)[141]

V.   Conclusion (Revelation 22:6-21)[142]

Of all the books written in the New Testament none of them

compares to Revelation. Revelation provides the Christian with a detail

account of prophecy concerning what is to come in the future.

Furthermore, Revelation is the final book written in the New Testament by

the Apostle John. This inspired book of prophecy was writing on the

---

[135] ibid
[136] ibid
[137] King James Version. Holy Bible Grand Rapids: Zondervan 2001
[138] ibid
[139] ibid
[140] ibid
[141] ibid
[142] ibid

island of Patmos. (Revelation 1:9)[143] Prophecy provides the Christian with a since hope. Without prophecy the correct priorities in and of a Christian life would be of no effect. (Burge, Cohick & Green, 2009 p. 432) The purpose of writing this book was to compile all prophetic truths of the Bible, and to answer all unanswered questions concerning the truths. Another purpose of composing was to encourage the people of God. Although, the Christians were under attack all must remain strong and vigilant. Persecution to the church was to be expected however, persecution cannot hinder nor destroy the Church of God or God's church. Christians today still have this blessed hope. Lastly, the composing of Revelation promotes godly living and well thought out living. The basic outline of this book reveals from within itself. (Revelation 1:19)[144] Many believe each verse to be "divine outline". (Benware 2003 p. 272)

The message of Revelation is revealed in the letters to the seven churches. The seven churches are the church of Ephesus; Smyrna; Pergamum, Thyatira; Sardis; Philadelphia; and Laodicea. The church of Ephesus is compliment by Christ in remaining steadfast to Him.

---

[143]ibid
[144] King James Version. Holy Bible Grand Rapids: Zondervan 2001

(Revelation 2: 1-7)[145] However, in their overcoming efforts Ephesus achieves through Christ. The Ephesians was encouraged to keep a repentant heart. The church of Smyrna is a church Jesus praised for their endurance. (Revelation 2:121-17)[146] Smyrna warned to be aware of idolatry although many were suffering from poverty conditions. The Pergamum's church included a group of loyal saints. (Revelation 2:12-17)[147] Though the church of Pergamum experienced spiritual hostility they remained committed and faithful. Because of their commitment and faithfulness Pergamum received a commendable for Christ. The Thyatira church is a church body of love, faith and diligence. (Revelation 2:18-29)[148] However, immorality seemed to be prevalent among this church family; but the believers received the "morning star" (Revelation 22:16)[149] Sardis, a church with little to no good present among the saints. The church of Sardis is known for spirituality but lack spiritual power. (Revelation 3:1-6)[150] Philadelphia received acknowledgements and or

---

[145] ibid
[146] ibid
[147] ibid
[148] ibid
[149] ibid
[150] ibid

recognition for a wavering faith. (Revelation 3:7-13)[151] The

Philadelphians are believers who are honored due their delight in the Lord.

The church of Laodicea was the worst church concerning spirituality of all

seven churches. Laodicea had no praise offered due to their indifferences.

Although Laodicea lacks spirituality they indeed posed material wealth

.The letters to the seven churches are accounts of how Christ came to save

the Christian church. Revelation gave special attention to the churches of

Asia. (Revelation 1:4)[152] Though each church differs, Christ love is shown

and revealed throughout all churches.

An area of significance in Revelation is the program of Christ

outline. (Revelation 4:1-22, 5)[153] In this portion of Revelation John begin

to describe his vision. The vision John describes comes into play once the

churches have been restored by Christ. The church had to be removed

before judgment is released upon this earth. The Apostle John begins to

write what he saw. John saw Christ as King coming to judgment and rule

the world. Therefore, Christ will then establish His kingdom. The vision

---

[151] ibid
[152] King James Version. Holy Bible Grand Rapids: Zondervan 2001
[153] ibid

reveals the throne of God which is the supreme authority of and over all things. Next, the vision presents the twenty four elders who are the churches and four living beings. The seal of scrolls was shown then the question was asked "who has authority to break the scroll seals?" Only Christ Jesus has the power to destroy the scrolls. And Christ will extinguish His judgment. (St. John 5:22, 26-27)[154] Upon the conclusion of the vision heaven rejoices. (Revelation 19:1)[155] The bride (church) is in heaven and she is being rewarded. The second coming of Christ is announced He then returns as triumph King of Kings.

In order to properly interpret Revelation an understanding of the Apocalypse must be understood. The Apocalypse is the prophetic term in reference to Revelation. Apocalypse allows a literal interpretation of the future as well as the present. The indoctrinate truth is reveal through the Apocalypse in Revelation. Revelation stands alone with the details it uncovers. Though the plan of Revelation is shown in symbols with interpretations to prophecy the hidden mystery of Christ's coming is unfold. Revelation the plan of God revealed to all. The Apostle John

---

[154] ibid
[155] ibid

prepares believers and unbelievers as to what is and what is to come.

God's plan was for man to live on earth in paradise. (Genesis 1-2)[156] Once

Christ conquers the world the saints of God will be able to enjoy

fellowship with God forever. Many saints of God have had to endure

hardships, persecutions, and mistreatment; but the joy awaits them in

heaven cannot be compared.

---

[156] King James Version. Holy Bible Grand Rapids: Zondervan 2001

Conclusion

Reflecting upon my life and its day to day living experiences, I do believe my life is a witnessing tool to all whom I encounter. While living in a world of uncertainty we must have a grip on life. One particular day coworker of mine was faced with hardships. She came to work in distressed, disgruntle, and mean. Due to her position in leadership she is forced to accommodate and or work with all personnel. Being lead of God, I went begin to converse with her. To my surprise, I was rejected that day. Feeling a level of disappointment and rejection one went an away sorrowful. On another day, I felt the unction to witness again to Lady A. Remembering the rejection pain day prior I was reluctant. The Holy Spirit impressed it upon me to mention something God has done. However, tears begin to fall from her eyes. She then begins to open up. I shared with her the plan of salvation. She then rededicated herself then and there to God.

Being lead of God an evangelist myself went on a faraway journey. While on this journey the evangelist met a man of great substance. Though the blessed man had no physical ailments there was something strange of this man. As the day progress, the blessed spoke and said I am so glad you stop to speak to me kind sir. The blessed man was suffering from neglect and a broken heart. What becomes of a broken heart? As we converse the blessed man realize that he had neglected the service of the Lord and the do diligence he once had for the local church. He then asks for prayer and I lead him through a rededication prayer.

It is safe to conclude that the work of an evangelist is never completed. Each day we as saved blood bought Christians live we must seek opportunity to witness to a dying world. Being a present day evangelist, I am encouraged to hold fast to my faith knowing there is no failure when an evangelist lean and depend on God. Evangelists must listen to the leading of the Holy Ghost to ensure the work of the ministry in evangelism is successful.

It is my belief that my struggle is relating to people in the "incarnational" level. Though, I am fully aware that we are God's representatives here on earth flesh can be a challenge. Incarnational means the doctrine that the second person of the Trinity assumed human form in the person of Jesus Christ and is completely both God and man.

Sin has left a guilty stain and Jesus has washed all our sin away. However, my sin is every before and many times I feel so unworthy to teach and or carry this good news. In addition, for the barriers to be removed in my life I will need to pray more. Praying more will allow one to commune with God the more. When one commune with God and learns he or she knows how to trust him more then all barriers and obstacles will be and shall be removed.

However, reflecting upon the statement, "dealing with lost people will cause us to get our hands dirty and sweaty just like tending to yard work." When considering this statement one is lead to reaffirm his or her call in the ministry of evangelism. There are those who do not know God or the power of salvation to a believer. Since there is a lack of knowing God to the unbeliever, work is necessary. When offering the unbeliever Christ his old nature wrestles with the new man. Whenever Christ is introduces something takes place to and with the unbeliever. First, the evangelist must ensure he or she are meek and lowly at heart. People know people; therefore genuineness can be felt. All have sinned and fall short of God's glory. Romans 3:23. The evangelist must remain approachable during and after his or her witnessing. There are no big "I" and little "you" in God. We all are saved and kept by God's grace. Practical expression is the only format in which people can see and know God is real and cares. Finally, one must reaffirm to the unbeliever that Jesus cares. Jesus proved how much he loved us when He died on Calvary. Whenever a friend is needed Jesus when be there like none other. For God is love the world that He gave His only begotten Son, that whosoever believed shall be saved. St. John 3:16[157]. An evangelist of Jesus Christ has been preconceived as being many things, however, he or she has the blessed hope of Jesus Christ. Though ideas and perceptions have been made, one must never be fearful of getting dirty. It is in the dirtiness when true deliverance takes place.

It is significant that man understands and realizes that God is involved and concern about all humanity. We as humans are more and much more than an evolved animal. There is no possible way for anyone to travel through life and not know God. Nature reveals to all intellectual beings that there is a loving God who is concern about His children. One can

---

[157] King James Version. Holy Bible Grand Rapids: Zondervan 2001

conclude that a personal relationship with God will enable a life of obedience with a heart for God and the things of God.

Reflecting upon my researches and studies of Genesis humanity has been favored and loved by Almighty God. Notice how the Trinity is revealed and shown in the following passages: Genesis 1:1[158]; Genesis 1:2[159]; Genesis 1:26, 32[160]; Genesis 3:15[161]. First, Genesis 1:1; reveals the authority of God the Father as creator. One can appreciate the vast work of God and how the Hebrew Bible (Old Testament) centers on Him. Next, Genesis 1:2; provides the revealing of the Trinity at work as the Holy Spirit is demonstrated. In this passage, the wind is revealing the breath of God as it permeates across the deep. In Genesis 1:26; 3:22, the Trinity can also be appreciated because God's power is shown; and God's goodness is seen. God is powerful due to the innateness to speak things into existence as "from nothing" (ex nihilo Latin derived) God is distinct from all His creation. God is good. God has a loving concern for His creation. Human beings are special; we are the handiwork of our Father and Creator –

---

[158] ibid
[159] ibid
[160] ibid
[161] ibid

created in his image and likeness. Though man is in God's likeness he is not and cannot ever be God. Man is placed on earth to subdue it, replenish it and rule over all living things. (Genesis 2:7, 21-22)[162] The Creator of all things loves and cherishes mankind. God is composed of physical and spiritual attributes; therefore making it possible for him identify with man. Intellect, emotions, and free will are what build the embodiments of a man. The heart reveals the emotions and sensual side of a man. God's Word demonstrate how God finds all He has done as good, and very good. Finally, Genesis 3:15[163]; offers the mercy of God to all. Creation suffering the grave consequences of sin however; God love has been extended. The serpent eats dirt and slides on his belly. Eve (the mother of all living) will labor. Adam (the father of all mankind) will labor too by the sweat of his brow.

The called of God are anointed to walk in the newness of our Lord. God has anointed us to be the light of this world and for our conversations to be seasoned. Psalm 23:5[164]; "Thou prepare a table in the presence of

---

162 King James Version. Holy Bible Grand Rapids: Zondervan 2001
163 ibid
164 ibid

mine enemies: thou anoint my head with oil; my cup runneth over." We are in a time and a season God is doing awesome things. Can you believe it? We are not just sitting by acting with the same old mindset. In order for us to reach our fullest potential a repositioning of mindset must take place. Therefore, the traditional mindset from the past that's was order and directed by man. God knows what is best for each of us and we have the anointing to move out and to walk upright. It is our job to work and operate with those whom God has given to us within this time and season. Jesus healed the blind, the sick and raised their dead. Mindset was change. The anointing destroys the yokes.

One need only look at a history book or text on human psychology to recognize that conflict, both internal and external, is a given in this world. Peace treaties bring only temporary resolution to ongoing conflict. A vacation on a tropical island may bring some relief to a stressed life but eventually the conflicts of everyday life return. It would be easy to fall prey to the belief that real peace is just not possible. And yet, Jesus said "I am leaving you with a gift – peace of mind and heart" (John 14: 27,

NLT)[165]. The peace He gives us most certainly is not like the kind of temporary peace of the world. His peace is the gift of a reconciled relationship with God. This is the peace Jesus demonstrated on the Cross as He fully submitted to the Father's divine plan. Psalm 22, beginning with that plaintive cry "My God, my God! Why have you forsaken me?" (Ps. 22:1, NLT)[166] clearly describes this supernatural peace as verses expressing physical and emotional struggle are overtaken by pronouncements of God's eternal love and gift of life through Christ. "For he has not ignored the suffering of the needy. He has not turned and walked away. He has listened to their cries for help" (Ps.22:24, NLT)[167].

One paraphrased translation of Jesus' promise to his disciples (and to us) describes the gift this way: "I'm leaving you well and whole. That's my parting gift to you. Peace. I don't leave you the way you're used to being left – feeling abandoned, bereft. So don't be upset. Don't be distraught" (John 14:27, The Message)[168]. The gift of peace Jesus offers us is found in His work on the Cross and our reconciled relationship with

---

[165] King James Version. Holy Bible Grand Rapids: Zondervan 2001
[166] New Living Translation Bible
[167] The Message Bible
[168] ibid

God. And if that were not enough, He promises to come back for us and gives us the Holy Spirit to keep us company in the between time! This is peace anchored firmly in our Eternal God and not the world – a peace that Paul exhorts "is far more wonderful than the human mind can understand. His peace will guard your hearts and minds as you live in Christ Jesus" (Phil. 4:7, NLT)[169].

Biblical wisdom and worldly wisdom are two forms of communication that is used daily by all persons. However, the driving force in which one uses is determines by his or her motivation. One account of biblical wisdom states "Revenge is mine saith the Lord." This account of biblical wisdom encourages believers to rest in the assurance that God will and can deliver all those whom put their trust in Him. On the other hand, worldly wisdom states "Get revenge on those who hurt you." Many individuals base their living off concepts such as get others before they get you. If persons seek to always get even then nothing in this life can be accomplished; therefore, worldly brings about more discord. One can conclude that worldly perspective offers a world of discord constantly and

---

[169] King James Version. Holy Bible Grand Rapids: Zondervan 2001

the biblical concept presents trust in Lord will handle the disheartening mistreatment one may feel.

To love God is to love Him with all your heart, mind, soul and strength which means a total surrender of your will to Him. It also leads us to love our neighbor as ourselves (Mark 12:30-31)[170]. "If a man say he loves God, and hate his brother, he is a liar-----"(1 John 4:20-21)[171]. Another important fact to look at is that after the resurrection, Peter announced to the other disciples that he was going fishing. After the disciples had spent night fishing, they caught nothing. When Jesus appeared they were able to catch fish. Jesus asks Peter repeatedly did he love him more than the Fishing business. Peter's response was first affirmative, but after Jesus pursued the questioning, Peter became grieved because he remembered his earlier failures. Here, Jesus was demanding from Peter the kind of love that would put God first and would produce unwavering loyalty and faithfulness. Loving God is to keep His

---

[170] New Living Translation Bible
[171] ibid

commandment (John 14:15)[172]. Being loyal, faithful and confident are also attributes of loving God.

In addition, keep in remembrance the synoptic gospels and their meaning understanding the gospels are not autobiographies of Christ. Their purpose is not to be autobiographies of Christ; his earthly life span was only 33 years of life. Christ provided man with everything he needs to live a successful Christ life; however He was still all God in the flesh. The gospels are written from the concept of how each saw and encounter Christ. Therefore, it is safe to say the viewpoint from Christ in which we read comes from the authors' development with miracles and teachings under the guidance of the Holy Spirit.

Matthew, prior occupation before coming to Christ and becoming a disciple was a tax collector. Tax collectors were not popular among the Jews. As a matter of fact, if one was a tax collector it was understood he was a cheat. One who abused others to receive his own fortune at the expense of others? It is no mystery Matthew had heard about Christ. Also, if a man a tax collector he had some form of knowledge; therefore he

---

[172] King James Version. Holy Bible Grand Rapids: Zondervan 2001

heard and knew of the Lord. But when he met the Lord forsook all and followed Jesus. Matthews's message was to the Jews to inform them that Christ the King of the Jews is King above all. Most importantly he provided them with information from Moses Law showing how Christ is the fulfilled manifestation of God.

Mark gives the evidence of how Christ is the Son of God. Then he goes a little deeper a shows how Jesus public success in Galilee and Judea. As one reads Marks' gospel one can see how he organizes the ministry of Jesus Christ. It is understood and recognized that Saint Mark wrote his gospel from Rome. Therefore, the gospel of Mark geared to the audience of the Romans. In researching the Romans one must keep in mind their stern desire to maintain order. Mark views our Lord as a Servant King. By showing the Jesus as serving King is depicting his humility that he will should among men. If one is to believe that Saint Mark is the source for Saint Matthews and Saint Luke then there must exist a wide range of these gospels. Mark was well known in Rome very rarely used concerning the gospel. Saint Mark, a follower of Christ turned things around in Rome at least offering those who desired a more excellence way.

Luke as in his counter brethren gives a similar but interesting depiction of our Lord. First, Luke sees the Lord God as a man. The Jesus proved himself to be all man but all God in the flesh. Jesus was revealed to be a man because of all he suffered and encountered as man. The uniqueness of Jesus Christ was how he conducted himself and distinguished him. Jesus' conduct and precepts revealed to men how one can be a devout follower of God in the flesh through Him. Saint Luke keys into this by recognize the Man make up. Luke was a physician by occupation. Understanding of Luke occupation gives one a deeper insight of how Luke sees our Lord. He is addressing the Greeks. In addition, he proves God's salvation sent through the Jews to the world in his messages. His made of objective was to allow all to know that God has revealed himself in Jesus Christ the fulfillment of himself in the flesh.

In each of the "synoptic gospel" listed above one can see the similar but differences in each of disciple's messages. Matthew, Mark, Luke are often referred to as the "synoptic gospels." The synoptic suggest that there is a literary form to each that is similar. Literary dependence means they are interconnected to each other. Their interconnection is mostly seen in the Greek translations more so then in other translations. Though there are historical criticism of the gospels we can rest assured that He lives and His words are still true and can be trusted.

When we became a Christian, God gave us spiritual sight and hearing so we could begin experiencing His presence and activity all around us. The Holy Spirit helps you to develop these spiritual senses as you walk with Him. Spiritual sensitivity to God is a gift that must be accepted and exercised. Scripture indicates that those who are spiritually dead cannot see or understand spiritual things (Matt. 13:14-15)[173]. Without spiritual eyes, you can be right in the midst of a mighty act of God and not recognize it.

There is a radical difference between seeing your surroundings from a human perspective and seeing life through spiritual eyes. Non-Christians will see world events around them and become confused. Believers will look at the same events, recognize the activity of God, and adjust your life to Him. When you meet an individual who is seeking God, you will recognize the convicting work of the Holy Spirit and adjust your

---

[173] King James Version. Holy Bible Grand Rapids: Zondervan 2001

life to God's activity (Rom. 3:11)[174]. Someone without spiritual perception will encounter that same person and not grasp the eternal significance of what is happening in that person's life. Others will hear of new philosophies and trends in society and not know how to discern the truth. You will hear God's voice over the noise of the world's voices, and you will keep your bearings in the midst of the confusing circumstances.

Sin dulls your senses, ultimately leaving you spiritually blind and deaf. Do not be content with merely seeing with physical eyes and hearing with natural ears but not sensing what God is doing. Ask God, through the power of the Holy Spirit, to sensitize you to His activity all around you.

The Bible is often taken for granted, even by those who vehemently support its inspiration and authority. Many believers associate Bible study with drudgery; limiting themselves to mere samples, they never cultivate a true taste for its contents. There are two basic reasons for this problem: lack of a proper method. This section is designed to overcome these obstacles to fruitful Bible study.

---

[174] ibid

To own a Bible is a tremendous responsibility—to whom much has been given, much is required (Luke 12:48)[175]. The Scriptures must not merely be owned, but known, but believed; not merely believed, but obeyed. To encourage this, we will look at the prerequisites, process, and practice of the Bible study.

THE PREREQUISITE OF A PLAN

Even if we realize the tremendous significant of a working knowledge of the Word in our lives, the prospect of Bible study may still seem unexciting and unrewarding because of the inadequate procedures we have used in the past. We may be properly motivated, but we could also be victims of improper methods. When people grope in the darkness of haphazard approaches to Scripture, it is little wonder that Bible study seems so unsatisfying and has such a minimal place in their lives. The hit and miss approach of Bible roulette provides little spiritual nourishment. Without an ability to understand and apply the truths of Scripture in a practical and meaningful way, believers miss out on the benefits of exploring and discovering biblical truths for themselves. This is why so

---

[175] King James Version. Holy Bible Grand Rapids: Zondervan 2001

many Christians have only a secondhand knowledge of the Bible and rely almost exclusively on the input of teachers and preachers. The material on the process and practice of Bible study in this handbook will provide you with a plan that makes your time in the Word more rewarding.

THE PREREQUISTE OF DISCIPLINE

While we need a plan or method of getting into Scripture for ourselves, no approach to the study of the Bible will be effective without a measure of discipline and consistency. If we are convinced of the value of time spent in the Word (the problem of motivation) and realize that fruitful approaches are available (the problem of method), the only remaining obstacle is the inertia that keeps us from beginning and tempts is to stop. There is no shortcut to extracting the deeper spiritual truths from the mind of Scripture. Even though they are available to all, we must be willing to expend the effort to find them. The dividends are well worth the effort: consistent time in the Word will shape the way we see the world and the way we live our lives. But this consistency cannot be won without commitment.

THE PREREQUISITE OF DEPENDENCE

We need a plan for bible study, and we need the discipline to follow through with that plan so that it will become a habitual part of our lives. But these will do us little good if they are not pursued with a conscious sense of dependence upon the reaching and illuminating ministry of the Holy Spirit (St. John 16:13-15)[176]. We must combine discipline (human responsibility) with dependence (divine sovereignty) as we approach the Scriptures. We cannot properly comprehend or respond to biblical truths in our power; this requires the grace of God.

In addition, a minister's job and or corner is never done however he or she will encounter Non-Christian as well as Christian and there are things and goals they must bear in mind to be effective in witnessing. When you became a Christian, God gave you spiritual sight and hearing so you could begin experiencing His presence and activity all around you. The Holy Spirit helps you to develop these spiritual senses as you walk with Him. Spiritual sensitivity to God is a gift that must be accepted and exercised. As the evangelist continues to walk in his or her calling lives will be change. They are yet walking in the newness of change and

---

[176] King James Version. Holy Bible Grand Rapids: Zondervan 2001

betterment. The Holy Scripture indicates that those who are spiritually dead cannot see or understand spiritual things (Matthew 13:14-15)[177]. Without spiritual eyes, you can be right in the midst of a mighty act of God and not recognize it. It has been and yet is my task to be a witness for the Lord. There is a radical difference between seeing your surroundings from a human perspective and seeing life through spiritual eyes. It is our jobs as evangelists and ambassadors for Christians to look through Christ's eyes. Non-Christians will see world events around them and become confused. You will look at the same events, recognize the activity of God, and adjust your life to Him. When you meet a person who is seeking God, you will recognize the convicting work of the Holy Spirit and adjust your life to God's activity (Romans 3:11)[178]. Those without spiritual perception will encounter that same person and not grasp the eternal significance of what is happening in that individual's life. Others will hear of new philosophies and trends in society and not know how to discern the truth. You will hear God's voice over the noise of the world's

---

[177] King James Version. Holy Bible Grand Rapids: Zondervan 2001
[178] ibid

voices, and you will keep your bearings in the midst of the confusing circumstances.

Therefore, the dulling noises of sin can weak and suffocate life out of all whom do not turn to Christ; ultimately leaving all spiritually blind and deaf. However, the minister cannot be content with merely seeing with physical eyes and hearing with natural ears but not sensing what God is doing and walk therein. I as an evangelist have learned to ask God, through the power of the Holy Spirit, to sensitize you to His activity all around you so that souls will be won for the kingdom.

Finally, theologians and other biblical writers offer suggestions to how God reveal himself to mankind. When desiring the knowledge of the Eternal One "Let not the wise man boast of his wisdom or the strong man boast of his riches, but let him who boasts about this: the he understands and knows me.'" (Jeremiah 9: 23-24)[179] Though many possess knowledge of godliness but yet have true sound knowledge of God. The human desire to recognize God is innate for them. Therefore, it is the incumbent of all humans to set themselves up to know and experience God. "This is eternal life: that they may know you, the only true God, and Jesus Christ,

---

[179] King James Version. Holy Bible Grand Rapids: Zondervan 2001

whom you have sent." (John 17: 3)[180] The Bible proves that there exist a

God and He is the only one God.   Perhaps steps of surrendering of oneself

should be implemented to assist in one quest for God. Steps of mediation

along with the self-denial will and can foster the ability to find God. Each

step of denial will reveal the true sincerity of a knowledge seeker whom

desires to know their maker. Over centuries past the study of God and God

being the One and only has been researched by many great leaders and

theologians. Due to God revealing Himself in those that believe with His

totality then it is indeed possible to know and experience the true and

living God, Jehovah. God is an amazing God, who is One and only; three-

in-one eternal. Since there is vastness in the world of changes with

challenges embracing God is not difficult. In knowing God, one has the

opportunity to see his or her self. Theologians give all to know that there

is a loving God whom desires to know His creation mankind. Humans

(man) have been created in the image of God; to worship God. There is no

great privilege than to know and appreciate Almighty God. One must seek

to lay hold to the God's wisdom through the word of truth the Bible.

---

[180] ibid

Ethical Census Report/ Questionnaire: Research Method

The method of choice for this ethical census involves an interview of all participates. After the interview has been conduct and the chosen personnel have been select then he or she will be given his or her duties. There has been an even number of equal genders and nationalities chosen to participate. However, each person is placed in different scenarios. Then, the selected personnel will gather all the data. The data collectors will complete the questionnaire to indicate his or her findings. Each participant is designate to be in certain region and demographic location. Therefore, data collectors will be assigned a location and will choose their designate at their locations of choice. This evaluation will be held at major events per the location of choice and or just from day to day activity. One will be able to conclude that Ministerial Ethics is a must in today's Western Culture and society.

Population

The population of people will focus on people at Church Offices and or Seminaries/ University on a daily bases. In each region there exist people whom interact with one another. The group interview of personnel will begin there day to day activities as usual within. 1st of the month and end of the month will be highlighted; for this times are the most challenging. Individuals will be coming requesting and or demanding services.

Sample

The sample will be conduct with seven chosen credential holders. He or she will chose the best time for them based on their region when to begin this research whether it is a major event being held or day to day use. The designee(s) will notate what he or she finds and observe.

Confidentiality

The data collector will give the participant a card so that he she can be notified after the research is complete. However, their privacy will be protected and he or she will not be exposing to the public and their information will remain undisclosed. In addition, they will already have received a form of privacy protection offered from the company/ agency to reassure the legitimacy of the research.

Questionnaire

Demographic Information:

Name:

For each of the following items, put an X beside the choice that best describes you:

1. Gender: Male   Female

2. Age: 18-20   18-20

              20-25   25>

3. Church Offices/ Seminary/ University used (please circle)

Checklist Items/Check each that applies:

4. I am a Pastor/Professor/ Teacher/ Counselor.

5. I am an Assistant/Volunteer/ Faculty Member.

6. I spend time in public ministry i.e. Outreach.

Likert Scale Items:

The following are statements that describe a school's curriculum. Read each statement and place a check in the box as to whether you strongly agree (SA), agree (A), are uncertain (U), disagree (D), or strongly disagree (SD) with each statement.

As a Clergyman/Biblical Counselor/Credential Holder: SA   A
     U   D   SD

7. I am saved.

8. I am a witness to others daily.

9. My life is a testimony to God's goodness.

10. My personality reflects my call in ministry.

11. When asked questions of integrity I am found morally upright.

12. My personal convictions are ethical in my daily practices.

Free Response Items:

13.   Is there anything you wish you would have been asked and wasn't?

_____

_____

_____

Bibliography

Dave Earley, David Wheeler. *Evangelism Is... How to Share Jesus with Passion and Confidence.* B & H Publishing Group, 2010.

David Wheeler, Vernon M. Whaley. *The Great Commission to Worship.* B & H Publishing Group, 2011.

—. *Worship and Witness - Becoming A Great Commission Worshiper.* LifeWay Press, 2012.

Dr. Jerry Pipes, Victor Lee. *Family to Famliy - Leaving a Lasting Legacy.* Jerry F. Pipes , 1999.

Edman, V. Raymond. *The Found The Secret.* Zondervan, 1960.

Fay, William. *Share Jesus Without Fear.* B & H Publishing Group, 1999.

III, Tremper Longman. *How To Read Genesis.* IVP Academic, 2005.

Oswalt, John N. *The BIble Among The Myths.* Zondervan, 2009.

Russie, Alice, ed. *The Essential Works of John Wesley.* Barbour Publishing, Inc., 2011.

Schaeffer, Francis A. *Genesis in Space and Time.* IVP Books, 1972.

Walton, John H. *Ancient Near Eastern Thought and the Old Testament.* Baker Academic, 2006.

—. *The NIV Application Commentary - Genesis.* 2001.

Weston, Anthony. *A Rulebook for Arguments.* Hackett Publishing Co. , 2009.

Will Mc Raney, Jr. *The Art of Personall Evangelism.* B&H Academic, 2003.

Wilson, Marvin R. *Perspectives on Our Father Abraham.* Wm. B.
Eerdmans Publishing Co., 2010.

Suheil, Laher. *Free Will and Determinism from a Scientific and Religious*

Perspective. Muslimmatters.org. Retrieved from

muslimmatters.org/2011/11/23free-will-and-determinism-frm-ascientific-

and-religious-perspective/

De Sousa, Avinash, Fruedian *Theory and Consciousness: A Conceptual*

Analysis, Men's Sana Monographs, Vol. 9(1), Jan-Dec 2011

AP Dijksterhuis and Loran Nordgren, *A Theory of Unconscious Thought*,

Social Association for Psychological Science Vol 1 (2), 2006

David, Hume. *The Obviousness of The Truth of Determinism. The*

Determinism and Freedom Philosophy Website. Retrieved from

http://www.ucl.ac.uk/uctytho/dfwDetHume.htm

Derk Pereboom. Meaning Life Without Free Will. *Determinism and*

Freedom Philosophy Website. Retrieved

ttp://www.ucl.ac.uk/uctytho/dfwVariousPereboom.htm

Lisa, Zyga. *Free Will is an Illusion*. PhysOrg .Retrieved from PhysOrg.com (2010)

Lawler, E. J., and Thye, S. R. *Bringing emotions into social exchange theory.* Annual Review of   Sociology, 25,pp.217-244. (1999).

Fowler, D. M., and Glenwright, B. J *Implications of Egalitarianism and Religiosity on Relationship Satisfaction. Interpersona.* Vol.7(2).215-226. Doi:10.5964/ijpr.v7i2.137.(2013).

Sprecher, S. *Correlates of Couples 'Perceived Similarity at the Initiation Stage and Currently. Interpersona.* Vol. 7(2).180-195. Doi:10.5964/ijpr.v7i2.1262013).

Firestoe, L. *How Your Attachment Style Impacts Your Relationship. Psychology Today*. Sussex Publishers, LLC (2013).

Social Psychology, Eighth Edition, by Elliot Aronson, Timothy D. Wilson, and Robin M. Akert. Published by Pearson. Copyright@2013 by Pearson Education, Inc

Sproul, R. *What Is The Gospel?* Retrieved August 19, 2014, from

http://www.ligonier.org/learn/articles/what-gospel/(2008).

McIntosh, G. L., & Rima, S. D. *Overcoming the dark side of leadership:*

How to become an effective leader by confronting potential failures (Rev.

ed.). Grand Rapids, MI: Baker. ISBN-13: 9780801068355 (2007).

Kouzes, J. M., & Posner, B. Z. *The leadership challenge* (4th ed.). San

Francisco: Jossey-Bass. ISBN-13: 9780787984922 (2008).

Ogden, G. *Unfinished business: Returning the ministry to the people of*

God (Rev. ed.). Grand Rapids, MI: Zondervan. ISBN-13: 9780310246190

(2003).

Connor, W. *Christian Doctrine* Nashville TN: Broad man Press\ (1937).

Morgan, G.C. *The crises of the Christ.* New Jersey: Fleming H. Revell.

(1936).

Moore, G.E. *Principia Ethica (1903)* Cambridge University Press revised

edition

ISBN 052144848)

Gutherie, S. *Christian Doctrine; Teaching of the Christian Church*. CLC Press (1968).

Grenz, S. *Theology for the community* Grand Rapids, MI: Eerdmans. (2000)

POLKINGHORNE, J. *The Trinity and an Entangled World: Rationality Physical Science and Theology* (2009).

PACKER, J.I. *Knowing God (1973).*

King James Version. Holy Bible Grand Rapids: Zondervan 2001

Placher, W. (Ed). *Essentials of Christian theology*. Louisville, KY: Westminster John Knox Press. (2003).

Alexander, P., & Alexander, D. *Zondervan handbook to the Bible* (4th ed.). Grand Rapids, MI: Zondervan. ISBN-13: 9780310331186 (Print text is required) (2011).

"Holman Bible Dictionary: Intertestamental History and Literature,"
http://www.studylight.org/dic/hbd/view.cgi?number=T3049

Carson, D., & Moo, D. *An introduction to the New Testament*. Grand Rapids, MI: Zondervan. ISBN-13: 978031023859 (2005).

Walton, John. H. *Ancient Near Eastern Thought and the Old Testament: Introducing the Conceptual World of the Hebrew Bible*. Grand Rapids, MI: Baker Academic, 2006. ISBN: 9780801027505.

Schaeffer, Francis A. Genesis in Space and Time. Downers Grove, IL: Intervarsity Press, 1972. ISBN: 9780877846369.

Made in the USA
Las Vegas, NV
27 July 2023

75326424R00115